"Shelley's real-world experie
fellow leaders when applying ... .
I'd had this leadership-development training twenty years ago."

— Ian M. Fletcher
Vice President, General Manager
ITW Global Tire Repair

"It was difficult to look in the mirror and realize I was teaching and managing well, but I was failing as a leader coach. To my great fortune, Shelley Hammell helped me reevaluate my approach as I entered an executive role for the first time, and the result has been nothing short of transformational for my leadership.

"Remarkably, it also led to transformation across my entire leadership team; as I began coaching with more thought and intention, my direct reports performed better and began coaching the leaders on their teams, and the chain reaction continues.

"As a bonus, the investment of initial time to coach has paid off in the long run, as leaders have become more deliberate, thoughtful, and self-sufficient, creating a culture where leaders and employees alike are more courageous in their day-to-day. Instead of spending my time teaching and making decisions for them, I'm able to coach and spend more time on the long-term strategy for our business, with the confidence needed to untangle myself from the weeds in which I was comfortable.

"I only wish I'd had this approach earlier in my career, and I encourage every leader to invest the time to learn how to REALLY coach!"

— Erin Lancaster McMillan
AVP – Customer Operations
Autotrader, Kelley Blue Book (Cox Automotive)

"Having spent more than three decades within the human resources discipline, leading people, processes, and organizational change, I am convinced that Shelley is one of the most impactful learning and development professionals I have ever had the pleasure to work with. Over the past several years, I have witnessed the positive impact Shelley has had on our organization, helping to foster personal skill development and professional growth within all levels of our management team.

"Through a leadership-development series that Shelley developed to address our specific concerns and needs, our organization has been able to begin to shift our culture and improve business outcomes. The SAGE Coaching Approach is something our leaders are immediately able to apply to empower and develop their teams.

"Shelley's techniques, tone, and style of facilitation, coupled with a deep subject matter expertise, have inspired an almost metamorphic change within some of our managers, supporting our business values by creating a behavioral environment that fosters personal accountability, ownership for outcomes, and engagement, particularly from those who have been exposed to this reflective development opportunity.

"I look forward to Shelley's continued support of our business, and our leaders, in the years to come."

— Ellen Duncan
SVP, Chief Human Resources Officer
InComm

YOU THINK YOU'RE COACHING, BUT YOU'RE *NOT!*

YOU THINK YOU'RE COACHING, BUT YOU'RE *NOT!*

How Great Leaders Build High-Performing Teams

SHELLEY HAMMELL

BOOKLOGIX·
Alpharetta, GA

ISBN: 978-1-63183-487-5 - Paperback
eISBN: 978-1-63183-488-2 - ePub
eISBN: 978-1-63183-489-9 - mobi

Library of Congress Control Number: 2019901476

Printed in the United States of America   021119

⊗This paper meets the requirements of ANSI/NISO Z39.48-1992 (Permanence of Paper)

DiSC® is a registered trademark of John Wiley & Sons, Inc. Herrmann Brain Dominance Instrument (HBDI)® is a registered trademark of Herrmann International. These properties are listed for exemplary purposes only. Neither the author nor the Sage Alliance is affiliated with the trademark owners.

You have brains in your head.
You have feet in your shoes.
You can steer yourself any direction you choose.
You're on your own. And you know what you know.
And YOU are the one who'll decide where to go . . .

Dr. Seuss, *Oh, the Places You'll Go!*

Table of Contents

Introduction

Coaching requires a change in how you think, behave, and interact with your team. When you learn to coach effectively, productivity rises, the team feels empowered, and engagement increases, leading to improved satisfaction and superior results for all stakeholders.

Many companies focus on building great leaders, but fail miserably in arming these leaders with the tools to be successful in our agile work culture. It is no wonder employee engagement is at a relatively low level (32 percent) in the US and (13 percent) globally, and has barely budged in over a decade.[1] It is also not surprising that managers feel less equipped than ever to influence the changes demanded by companies to grow high-performing, highly engaged teams that consistently achieve exceptional results.

Employees are being stretched beyond their means and being asked to do things in which they may have no experience. As a result, they fear they will make an inexorable mistake, one that will permanently tarnish their reputation and career trajectory. They feel unfulfilled and disconnected from the organization's larger strategy and mission. They are juggling a multitude of tasks and only receive recognition when they sacrifice their personal time to complete these tasks.

Managers, too, have enormous weight on their shoulders to meet increasing demands. They consistently find themselves being mere taskmasters who operate with limited resources and enormous time constraints, juggling a jam-packed calendar and vying priorities. With this as a backdrop, finding time to coach can be a very real challenge that simply eludes managers. Therefore, we see the perpetuation of the manager/trainer/boss trying their best to get the most out of disengaged employees to accomplish the obligatory goal only for the glory of doing it all again with the next initiative.

With the focus on performance and action, there is limited time to invest in developing skills that will prepare the employee for the next stage in their career. It is common practice to teach employees on the job. Upon completion of a task, there's always another one waiting in the wings, with more demands and even greater time constraints. With fluid roles, changing priorities, and focus on action, employees are burned out and not able to give their all.

Clearly, this operating model has to change.

My Wake-Up Call

Several years ago, as a vice president of global marketing, I flew to the South of France to brief some industry analysts on the direction of our company and the new enhancements to our products. Although not the reason most people go to the South of France, I was looking forward to my sojourn to the elite town of Marseille, where the best of the best of Parisian high society vacation.

As I stood at baggage claim, I could already feel a change come over me. I was in paradise. I saw the landscape through the front door of the airport. While inside, women, dressed smartly in their cool linen pants, adorned with expensive jewelry, perfectly coiffed hair, and expertly applied faces, stood alongside me. Similarly, distinguished men, in their white linen pantsuits and butter-soft leather loafers, sans socks, peppered the landscape. I was among the elite of French society, but something wasn't right. A feeling came over me, but I just couldn't put my finger on it.

As I attended my meetings and enjoyed some free time to explore the quaint village of Marseille, I became more in touch with my emotions. Despite my years with the organization, and my rapid rise to executive management, I felt I was a misfit. I didn't belong. It had nothing to do with my place in society, nor my place in the organization. Rather, it had to do with me. For years, I thought that climbing my way to the top, and leading one successful initiative after another, would define me as a leader. I had it all wrong. This wasn't what I was meant to be doing. I felt unfulfilled and had a burning desire to do more.

Suddenly, it came to me: my passion was developing people, not marketing campaigns. I recognized managers were ill-equipped with how to get the most out of disengaged employees. I had always been the one people came to for help in difficult situations. Developing, motivating, and engaging people was intuitive for me. I realized there was something in me I hadn't tapped into yet.

My time in the South of France proved to be a turning point in my career. After a rewarding career in sales and marketing, I took the leap and started my own executive coaching and leadership development company, and I've never looked back. Coaching is something I had always done innately, as a leader. I built this business based on my firsthand experience, with deep insight of what it takes for great leaders to become even more successful.

When I landed one of my first clients and saw them struggling with developing their leaders, I realized how much I could help organizations by coaching their leaders to be great coaches. As I reflected on their challenges, I noted this required a landmark approach to ensure the success of the leader, the team, and the organization.

Growing leaders has always been a passion of mine. As the vice president of marketing of a technology company, leading a high-performing team was my primary focus. As I gained greater responsibility and managed larger teams, I found it was imperative to develop each employee on my team, through engagement, empowerment, ownership, and accountability. It wasn't enough to meet deadlines; I wanted to ensure my team saw me as a leader who would help them grow. Throughout my career, I had been modeling this approach, but I had not developed it into something I could share with others.

Once I realized my new focus, I fervently documented the steps I intuitively took to develop and empower my teams. Through several iterations, the SAGE Coaching Approach was born. Over nearly a decade, I have coached numerous corporations and organizations to implement the SAGE Coaching Approach with their leadership teams, and all have experienced remarkable results.

Your Wake-Up Call

As a manager, you might be receiving satisfactory results from your employees, which might make trying a new approach to team development and engagement a low priority. The time you invest in training, meetings, and juggling changing demands leaves you little room to lead the way you want to. And having to micromanage, handhold, get in the trenches, and referee team members is beyond frustrating. Yes, you have been managing, but have you been coaching?

Want to gain commitment, engagement, ownership, and accountability from your team? Want to witness increased performance and improved outcomes? This starts with you. You need to show your team that you are willing to press the pause button on the distractions that stand in the way of their (and your) success, and the success of your entire organization. It is time you learned a comprehensive approach to transform yourself into a leader coach.

Coaching enables you to help your team consistently reach greater levels of performance and outcomes. Now is the time for your wake-up call.

Coaching requires a change in how you think, behave, and interact with your team. When you learn to coach effectively, productivity rises, the team feels empowered, and engagement increases, leading to improved satisfaction and superior results for all stakeholders.

It's a Win-Win

This is your time to understand how to move from satisfactory results to a high-performing team that delivers exceptional results, all through coaching. Through the simple yet landmark approach shared in this book, you will transform from a manager into a great leader by learning to coach your team. No matter your level within your organization, you have a great opportunity to grow as a leader while growing the leadership on your team.

This book will show you how to develop your team while simultaneously focusing on your own growth. This is an investment in your future as a leader, and the future of your team to develop them as stronger leaders. Coaching is how great leaders build high-performing teams.

For over a decade, I have shared this foolproof coaching approach with thousands of leaders in a variety of business sectors across the globe, who initially proclaimed they were coaching their teams. Only after our work together did they realize they had not been coaching at all. Instead, they had been directing the activities of the team to reach an outcome, but they had not been helping each employee to develop strong decision-making skills, take ownership, accept accountability, and grow into better leaders themselves.

This is a real-world approach that all leaders can immediately apply, in sales, marketing, customer service, operations, IT, and finance, and as presidents, vice presidents, directors, general managers, and human resources professionals. I call it SAGE:

- **S**ituation Analysis
- **A**lternatives and Options
- **G**oal Setting
- **E**xecution and Accountability

The SAGE Coaching Approach helps you uncover the root cause of a situation to ensure you and the employee are focused on solving the true challenge. Employees are empowered to confidently make tough decisions by learning how to weigh pros and cons and committing to the needed action. This inspires the team to take ownership, execute successfully, and remain accountable when faced with ambiguity and uncertainty.

You will get the most out of this book by reading each chapter in order, and completing the included exercises. Even if you think you know a particular step, I encourage you to read each one anyway. The chapters build on one another and include several tools and techniques to help you be a better coach and, in turn, be a great leader. This is also a useful guide for anyone who needs a refresher on any of the steps, or who wants to take their mastery to the next level.

The SAGE Coaching Approach is something you can immediately apply. The challenge of being a great leader coach is it takes practice. Most leaders discover that coaching is much harder than they ever thought. That's because this requires your commitment to change how you interact with your team. Fortunately, I have shown innumerable managers how to be successful leader coaches, and you are about to learn from that experience and, in turn, elevate your leadership profile while engaging and empowering your team.

It is time to help your team be more effective. It is time to advance your own leadership. Coaching is a win-win proposition that enables you to do both. Let's get started.

Laying the Foundation

You're Not Leading If You're Not Coaching

Learning to coach (and not just lead) helps you enhance your influence even further. You likely consider yourself a leader, but are you a coach? Learning to be a leader coach will improve your, and your team's, performance and help you achieve your business goals.

Gone are the days when teams were built with fixed job descriptions in mind. Today, teams are built with agile and flexible people who can apply their skills to a variety of demands that continue to evolve over time.

As a leader, when you see your team struggling, what do you do? With the precious resource of time, do you invest it in coaching your team? It is easy to fall into the trap of showing your team how to do the task with the belief that you are coaching them. As a leader, you may not be using your time wisely to coach your team and prepare them for the next challenge.

It used to be when an employee was struggling, regardless of the challenge, organizations would recommend additional training. But training can become a mere bandage to cover greater issues that need to be addressed. Training has its place, but when it becomes the default, it illuminates an opportunity for you as a leader. You have to take responsibility and coach your team.

You're a Manager, but Are You a Coach?

When a leader coaching approach becomes pervasive at all levels of an organization, from middle management up to the C-suite, everyone wins—the leader coach, the employees, the organization, and all of its stakeholders.

The top three outcomes for those who receive coaching are improved communication skills (42 percent), followed by enhanced self-esteem/self-confidence (40 percent) and increased productivity (39 percent). In fourth place is optimizing individual/team work performance (38 percent).[1] Coaching is a huge opportunity to develop leaders, improve performance, and position employees for the next step in their careers.

Coaching is collaborative. It is a partnership entered into by both you, the leader, and your direct report to build capabilities that will result in an agreed-upon outcome. Performance is enhanced by enabling your employees to try different approaches to see what works best for them. The leader coach provides feedback and insight along the way to help employees make real progress. This approach helps employees make the necessary behavioral shifts that close gaps and blind spots, and optimize strengths.

Coaching provides individualized attention, enabling employees to zero in on the competencies and the associated behavioral changes that will make them more effective. As a result, employees develop interpersonal skills, the softer side of leadership. These skills—including but not limited to speaking up in meetings, forming concise communications, gaining visibility, and increasing one's influence—are all areas you as the leader can help them address through a coaching approach. Employees become more agile and flexible as needs in the organization continue to evolve and change.

Learning to coach (and not just lead) helps you enhance your influence even further. You likely consider yourself a leader, but are you a coach? Learning to be a leader coach will improve your, and your team's, performance and help you achieve your business goals.

More and more leaders see the value of a coaching approach and are positioning this as a means to help their teams develop additional leadership skills and become more agile.

Invest in Your Greatest Asset, Employees

In chapter 3, you will learn the SAGE Coaching Approach, a comprehensive yet effective means to elevate you as a leader coach. For now, here are key outcomes of an effective coaching strategy, and how they can influence your team's productivity and impact your company's profits:

Increased employee engagement. Engaged employees are enthusiastic, motivated, and committed to give their best for the organization's success. Employee engagement accounts for many positive organizational outcomes, including decreased absenteeism, lower turnover, and higher productivity.

A sizeable number of organizations (65 percent) aim to expand the scope of managers/leaders using coaching skills in the next five years. Organizations that have strong coaching cultures are more likely to have high rates of employee engagement and strong revenue growth. When companies invest in the growth of an individual's leadership skills, employees respond by being more engaged in the organizational goals, they take greater ownership of their own roles, and they see the value of their contribution to the team's outcomes. This leads to higher performance and earnings.[2]

Greater employee empowerment and productivity. Empowered employees feel a great sense of autonomy in their work, know that their job has meaning and aligns with their values, are competent in their abilities, and believe they can make a difference. They are more likely to be confident employees who are committed to meaningful goals and demonstrate initiative and creativity to achieve them. Empowered employees trust their leaders and are more likely to put in the extra effort.[3]

When empowerment is low, only 4 percent of employees are willing to give the extra effort, but 67 percent are willing when empowerment is high. Higher empowerment translates to higher productivity.[4]

Engaged and empowered employees do more than what is required because of the investment you make in coaching them. They are tireless, energized, and willing to do whatever it takes to overcome obstacles and navigate complexity. Empowering your team demonstrates they are valued, you trust their judgment, and you are willing to invest in them through coaching. When productivity improves, the entire team and company realize tremendous benefits including increased loyalty, satisfaction, innovation, and profitability.

Heightened employee inspiration, engagement, and innovation. Making the time to coach motivates and inspires employees. That value translates to greater engagement and innovation.

Employees who spend an optimal number of hours (six hours per week) interacting with their direct leader are 29 percent more inspired, 30 percent more engaged, 16 percent more innovative, and 15 percent more intrinsically motivated than those who spend only one hour per week.[5] Coaching is a critical tool for leaders to engage and empower their teams, yet it is severely underutilized, with 20 percent of leaders spending only three to four hours, per *month*, coaching.[6] In fact, leaders need to spend more time coaching, as much as 40 to 50 percent.[7]

Coaching challenges your employees to anticipate trends, think strategically, and be more innovative. This is critical for teams with opposing demands and taxing deadlines to feel inspired and meet their goals. When you lead by coaching, your employees are able to take on new challenges that push them out of their comfort zone.

Increased employee satisfaction and retention. Coaching is the differentiator for employee satisfaction and retention.

More than 60 percent of employees who report to managers who are not good coaches considered quitting, versus 22 percent who report to the best managers.[8] When you coach your team, they appreciate the investment you make in them to help sharpen their skills. Satisfaction increases, and they feel more valued, which translates into greater loyalty and lower turnover.

When coaching is at the core of your leadership, employees strive to do their best. They desire to remain at their current position to make a greater impact and then to progress further in the company, rather than exit to find better, more rewarding opportunities elsewhere. Their loyalty stems from your investment and encouragement, which has a positive impact on employee retention.

Increased profitability. Finally, with all the benefits of coaching, your organization will see improvements to its bottom line.

Organizations that are the best in engaging their employees achieve earnings-per-share growth that is more than four times that of their competitors. Companies with highly engaged workforces realize substantially better customer engagement, higher productivity, better retention, fewer accidents, and 21 percent higher profitability.[9]

Organizations that have strong coaching cultures experience

above-average earnings as compared to those companies that do not engage in coaching. Even a 10 percent increase in employee productivity would double the profits of most organizations.[10] The connection is real between coaching and profitability.

Coaching truly is a game changer for optimizing leadership and building high-performing teams. It is also clearly a critical factor for companies that wish to positively impact their bottom line. Coaching is an essential part of leadership, and should be implemented at every level for organizations that wish to experience exceptional business results.

A New Perspective

For you, your team, and your organization to realize these benefits, it is vital to understand the distinction between what coaching is and what coaching is not.

In the below list, place a check mark in each box next to the role or roles that qualify as coaching:

- ☐ Advisor
- ☐ Instructor
- ☐ Teacher
- ☐ Facilitator
- ☐ Boss
- ☐ Supervisor
- ☐ Manager
- ☐ Mentor
- ☐ Sounding Board
- ☐ Leader

Now, let's explore each of these roles to determine if it qualifies as coaching.

Advisor

At first blush, this seems like the quintessential definition of a coach. However, philosophically, this is the true difference between what coaching is and is not. When you give advice, you are telling someone what to do.

As an advisor, you have positioned yourself as an expert on a specific topic. If you have ever found yourself saying, "Have you thought of this?" or "You should try this," you are giving advice and not coaching. You have a lot of experience as a leader, and as such you want to help an employee solve a tough problem. To successfully coach, you need to stop yourself from recommending ways the employee can approach or solve the problem. After all, what worked for you may not work for them.

I have seen employees come up with new and improved ways to solve a problem when given the chance to leverage their own creativity. Undoubtedly, you have experienced this as well. You must give employees the latitude to explore different options and perspectives to arrive at their own creative solution.

Telling the employee which path they should follow is not coaching. It is advising. That is not to say there aren't times when you will provide advice. In fact, as a manager, there are times when you will need to do just that.

Instructor

When you instruct, you command or direct the activities of others. This is not coaching. Instructing is when you give someone an order on what specifically needs to be done. You control the outcome by telling the employee what they need to do and, in most cases, how to do it.

Think about the instructions you get with a new assemble-your-own-furniture kit. Everything is spelled out, to the letter, of how to assemble the table or chair. Miss putting a screw in its place, the table or chair cannot possibly be sound. You must follow the step-by-step instructions to ensure you have done everything properly. And if you need to build another table or chair, you will need to follow the directions, all over again, or miss doing this correctly.

There are times when you may need to direct an employee to do something, such as fulfilling a specific directive from higher-level leadership. Your job as a manager is to satisfy this request, but this does not constitute coaching.

Teacher

A teacher imparts knowledge. My high school Italian teacher took a genuine interest in helping me learn the language, as I stumbled at pronouncing fundamental sounds. You may think fondly of teachers who made a big impact on your life as well. They may have been focused on inspiring you to learn something new and see the possibilities of learning. But teaching, in its rudimentary form, is not coaching.

When you teach, you convey information and share your knowledge to help others master a skill you know well. There are instances when you must teach a new skill or convey knowledge to help an employee on your team learn, just as my high school Italian teacher did for me. But that is not coaching.

Facilitator

A facilitator is someone who helps to bring about an outcome through their guidance. Yes, this is coaching. The job of a facilitator is to challenge others to think about different ways to accomplish a task, or to think about a problem from a different perspective.

When you serve as a facilitator, you are focused on helping the employee reach an agreed-upon outcome. A great leader knows how to progress these conversations with their employees. Through brainstorming and looking at different perspectives, you help the employee uncover the various ways to reach the end result. A facilitator is not focused on the right answer, but rather on exploring the different pathways to arrive at the answer. A leader coaching approach can help you do just that.

Boss

A boss is the person in charge, someone who gives orders in a domineering manner. You guessed it—not a coach.

The term boss is loosely used to designate the individual someone reports to. And on your team, that is you. Think about how this term is often used. It usually sounds something like this: "The boss said we need to do this."

As a leader coach, you empower your team to reach an outcome, but you do not dominate the conversation and give orders on how to get there. There are times when you need to give an order and tell your team what to do, but that does not epitomize a coaching approach.

Supervisor

A supervisor oversees and monitors employees to ensure their tasks are completed. In a coaching approach, reaching the outcome happens through engagement and empowerment, not through regulating the work to ensure tasks are successfully completed. A laser focus on monitoring a task is not coaching.

Manager

There has been an abundance of books written on the topic of whether a manager is a leader and the difference between the two. Here, I am making the distinction as well, but with a leader coaching approach in mind. Although the term is often used broadly, a manager is responsible for *controlling* or administering a set of business activities. The idea of controlling suggests checking one's work or verifying accuracy, through evidence. This is not a leader coaching approach.

Managing is a rigid approach to ensuring policies and procedures are met. Following policies and procedures is important, but that is not coaching. You may use the term manager, but to fall under the moniker of great leader, you must leverage a coaching approach.

Mentor

Often the terms mentor and coach are used interchangeably; however, the roles have some noticeable differences. Mentorship takes place outside the formal manager relationship. Typically, a formal mentor has knowledge in a specific area of expertise. It may be functional expertise, such as finance or operations, or to help an employee master a specific skill such as public speaking. As a mentor, you serve as a role model who will, based on your experience, share your insight in a key area or skill set. As venerable as mentorship is, it is not coaching.

When you start a sentence with "Here's what I would do" or "Here's how I would do it" or "Here's how I have handled those situations in the past," you are most likely mentoring and not coaching.

Sounding Board

Let's get clarity on what a sounding board is before we determine if this is coaching. According to Merriam-Webster.com, a sounding board is a person or a group on whom one tries out an idea or opinion as a means of evaluating it. This is unquestionably coaching.

Not to be confused with giving advice, a sounding board is very different. When you act as a sounding board, you listen to the situation at hand, stimulate different perspectives, enable the employee to explore options, and provide encouragement to follow through.

You provide a safe place where employees can gain feedback on an idea, a recommendation, or a solution. A leader coaching approach helps an employee reach a solution or goal by talking through different alternatives and options, and evaluating them for viability, with you as the sounding board.

Leader

Coaching *is* strong leadership. You cannot deliver on business results without developing the talent on your team. An organization is made up of people. Your ability to motivate, engage, and empower your employees to reach their full potential is what helps you accomplish your goals, and is what makes you a great leader. This is accomplished through a leader coaching approach.

Great leaders are focused on making more great leaders. To accomplish this, you must give your team an opportunity to learn and develop while providing a safe place for them to take risks and make mistakes. This shows you are willing to invest in them and you have their back.

As you can see, a leader wears many hats and has vast responsibilities. This book is dedicated to becoming an effective leader coach, with the understanding you have to juggle countless other roles, many of which are depicted here.

Not All Leaders Are Great Coaches

Coaching is an approach that enables you to achieve more through others by optimizing both their performance and their potential, and at the same time sharpening your leadership capabilities. It is an intentional approach that helps employees make the tough calls, be more decisive, and develop into stronger leaders.

Not all leaders are great coaches; however, great coaches *are* great leaders. The focus of this book is to help you implement the SAGE Coaching Approach to elevate your team from ordinary to extraordinary performance. Become an even better leader by becoming a great coach and building a high-performing team.

As you read on, you will discover how the SAGE Coaching Approach contributes to your effectiveness as a leader. Once you begin practicing these techniques, you will see that they empower your team to optimize their performance, look at different perspectives, be more confident decision makers, and overcome obstacles, all while taking ownership and action.

The benefits you and your team will experience are immeasurable and ultimately rewarding. The value of using the SAGE Coaching Approach is infinite. In the chapters that follow, we will explore the key qualities of being a leader coach. You will gain an understanding of how to overcome the obstacles that stand in the way of developing yourself and your team into stronger, more effective leaders.

Your Call to Action

Reflections I Will Make

Which of the following roles do you want to focus on first? Check as many as apply.

- ☐ Advisor
- ☐ Instructor
- ☐ Teacher
- ☐ Facilitator
- ☐ Boss
- ☐ Supervisor
- ☐ Manager
- ☐ Mentor
- ☐ Sounding Board
- ☐ Leader

Actions I Will Take

1. As you reflect on your leadership, describe an example(s) where you demonstrated the roles you checked from the list. In what situations do you believe demonstrating these roles is effective? In what situations do you need to demonstrate less?

2. If you asked your team to rate you on the degree to

which you display these roles, how do you think you would score?

3. Which of these roles do you believe are your biggest challenge to overcome to be a great leader coach?

Go to www.thesagealliance.com/worksheets to download the following worksheet that will help you chart your progress.

When I Think I'm Coaching, but I'm Not
Evaluation

Evaluate your use of each of these roles in the interactions with your team.

Roles	Most Effective	Least Effective
Advisor		
Instructor		
Teacher		
Facilitator		
Boss		
Supervisor		
Manager		
Mentor		
Sounding Board		
Leader		

What three things will I *continue* to leverage as a leader coach?

1. _____

2. _____

3. _____

What three things will I do *differently* to improve as a leader coach?

1. _____

2. _____

3. _____

www.thesagealliance.com

Transform from Manager to Leader Coach

Leadership coaching personalities can be defined by four distinct styles. No one style is better than another, but it is beneficial to identify your style to help you determine which qualities or traits will help you be most effective, and which may render you less effective.

Today's dynamic business environment requires employees to make decisions quickly, often without a plan of how to get there. Employees are required to be more flexible. Fixed job responsibilities are a thing of the past. Employees are now required to leverage pervasive skill sets as priorities and demands continually change.

Employees are asked to take on a diverse set of work tasks with increased responsibilities—responsibilities that may not be core to their original role or strengths—with little or no direction. This pushes them outside of their comfort zone when they are expected to perform at the highest levels. The impact on the team is uncertainty, lower performance, and loss of confidence. The result for the company is lower productivity, high employee turnover, and lower bottom-line profits.

Coaching Is a Game Changer

If you are like most leaders, the amount of work set before you is a greater challenge than in the past. Everything is a priority, which can leave developing your team as an afterthought. However, this is exactly why becoming a leader coach is so critical to your success. Your team needs your help so they can adapt to the changing workplace.

Coaching is a game changer that will transform your leadership and help your team grow, thereby helping you establish a strong bench of high-performing leaders. Through your coaching, employees gain greater confidence, become more decisive, take ownership, and learn how to navigate the company's dynamic and changing culture. You optimize the performance of the team, enabling them to take on greater and more complex challenges and deliver on their commitments. In turn, this enhances your impact as a leader.

As you can see in the first scenario, when a leader tells, instructs, and advises, the employee is merely following direction. They take action on the *order* they were given and do as they were told. They are not empowered to make decisions and take the necessary actions without the leader's input.

The second scenario illustrates a leader coaching approach where you and your employee collaborate to solve critical business problems. You are a sounding board where conversation flows both ways. Both you and the employee engage in brainstorming, feedback is shared, and the employee is empowered to take decisive action. They learn how to be flexible in changing situations and gain confidence while doing so. In turn, they are better positioned to tackle future challenges autonomously.

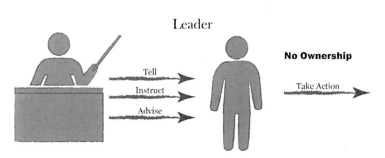

Leader Coach

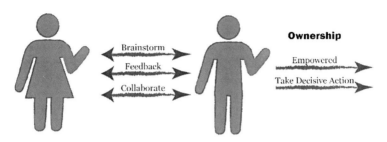

So, how do you transform your leadership style to that of a leader coach? You begin by acknowledging that the traditional approach to leadership does not work in today's agile workplace. You accept that there is always room for improvement in the way you lead. You remain focused on the goals and expectations of the company, and how your team can positively impact those goals. You commit to becoming a leader coach to empower your employees to become great leaders themselves. You reflect, practice, evaluate, and revise your leader coaching approach for maximum results.

You begin where you are today.

As with most high-performing leaders, you think you're coaching your team, but you're not! Your employees do what you want them to. They come to you when they are uncertain on how to proceed. You have an open-door policy and are willing to listen and advise them when they hit a roadblock. But does that make you a great coach? This might make you a good manager and teacher, but that does not constitute being a leader coach.

A leader coach recognizes there are many ways to reach a successful outcome and provides employees with the tools to make tough decisions on their own. This can, at times, require more trial and error on the part of the employee as they navigate ambiguous and complex situations. However, this raises the employee's confidence level and empowers them to make decisions not only today but in the future as issues arise, without having to check with you first. This eliminates the need for you to be at the heart of all decisions.

Leadership is about developing more leaders and having a strong leadership bench for those who can follow in your footsteps. You do this through a coaching approach. In the fast-paced environment in which you work, you have limited time to get your work done, which means coaching can fall by the wayside. When you become a leader coach, employees see the investment you make in them. As a result they are more engaged, leading to high-performing teams that deliver superior outcomes.

As you adopt a coaching approach, you learn to understand the employee's motivations, desires, and challenges. Armed with this understanding, you tailor your coaching approach to help your team reach their full potential. This includes championing them to make tough decisions, execute successfully, and remain accountable, all the while helping them adapt to become flexible and agile leaders who perform at the highest levels.

You Think You're Coaching: Sara's Story

In the seven years Sara has been with her company, she has worked her way up and earned a coveted spot on the executive team. As part of the leadership team for the past four years, she knows how important outcomes and results are to the organization. She has a seasoned team and she feels confident as a leader, but she knows there is room for improvement.

Sara needs her team to be more independent and resourceful in making decisions, and more innovative in responding to customer and market needs. Over the past two years, the workload has increased substantially, and Sara has been unable to hire additional resources. Recently, she realized the outcomes of her team do not reflect their capabilities. They are not performing at the highest level possible, and she's concerned this may be a reflection on her leadership.

In meetings with her team, she has shared feedback regarding their priorities. She has spent time showing them ways to be more resourceful and advising them how to prioritize innovation to meet customer needs. These conversations have been time consuming, with little change in the team's effectiveness.

Sara is puzzled by how to fix this situation. She believes she has inherently good people who are becoming increasingly overwhelmed with changing priorities and a mounting workload, leaving little time for strategic thinking and innovation. She knows she must do something differently.

Typically, she reviews her expectations with the team. She shares her recommended course of action and outlines the parameters. She expects her team to execute successfully on the activities she has spelled out and plans to check in with them to chart their progress. Expectations for results at the company are high. Because of the high visibility, demanding deadlines, and formidable expectations, her team works through the various initiatives and does all they can to juggle the numerous deadlines.

When the team uncovers a challenge, they come to Sara for advice. She is quick to jump in, remove any roadblocks, and fix areas that have gone off course. This enables the team to get back on track and satisfy another priority.

> Sara realizes she needs a better way to work with her team and help them realize their full potential while still meeting the company's goals.

Change Your Approach

You may be in Sara's situation. Perhaps you are doing everything you know to bring out the best in your team and position them for success. Yet, you wonder why they are not performing at higher levels, why they are not solving problems on their own, why they always need your help and advice at each stage. You labor to stay afloat amid high expectations matched with unrelenting workloads, tight deadlines, and overwhelmed employees. You are certain your team has what it takes to perform well, be innovative, and think strategically. So how can you bring about these results as a leader?

Being a great leader requires you to take a fresh look at your approach to leading your team. Perhaps, like Sara, you need to shift from directing the solution, advising your employees, and telling them how to do things, to focusing on empowering your team to reach the desired outcome, with your guidance. A transition to a strong coaching culture requires a change in management style. The most effective management style can be summed up in four words: coaching, collaborative, supportive, and participative.[1]

This requires you to transform from a manager into a leader coach. The very nature of a coaching approach inherently positions you to empower your employees to be more flexible while reaching their goals and ensuring the work gets done. As a leader coach, you encourage employees to take initiative, make the tough calls, execute, and remain accountable for their commitments. This ensures you are developing a strong leadership bench.

The transformation is dramatic with your team, and you elevate your leadership as a result.

They move from this . . .	To this
Lack of confidence making critical decisions.	Increased confidence making complex decisions, even when faced with ambiguity.
Seeing the manager as the go-to for final approval or decision making.	Being empowered to make critical decisions without running them by the manager first.
Relying on the manager to take the lead, driving initiatives and decisions forward.	Achieving outcomes seamlessly with the employee committed to take the necessary risks, despite obstacles.
Feeling lack of ownership and accountability toward an initiative.	Following through and remaining accountable, taking the risk for ramifications associated with tough decisions.
A team of inflexible, tactical doers.	A confident and engaged leadership bench that is agile and flexible in the face of changing priorities and job requirements.
Overwhelmed and focused on executing the next project or imminent deadline.	Committed to taking initiative, going the extra mile, and achieving outcomes with unsurpassed results.
Disengaged and disempowered.	More satisfied and engaged, feeling part of the team and connected to the organizational purpose by adding value.
Waiting for the manager to check in to solve all their challenges.	Solving challenges on their own, and remaining focused on what matters for the team and the company.

The transformation shifts focus from doing to achieving with a sense of ownership and purpose.

Time to Look in the Mirror

No two leaders are alike. You have different skills, experiences, and people who have influenced your career. Likewise, different leaders have different coaching styles. Before we explore the SAGE Coaching Approach, take a moment to reflect on your leader coaching style.

If you have taken an industry assessment, consider the common themes and what they reveal about your leadership style. There are many personality and leadership assessments available on the market. A few recommendations include the Herrmann Brain Dominance Instrument (HBDI), DiSC, the Hogan Assessments, and the Birkman Method. Assessments are designed to provide you the needed insight into your leadership style. By gaining this insight, you will understand how your style influences your effectiveness as a leader coach.

The following Leader Coach Assessment will highlight your strengths and bring clarity to areas that will come more naturally, as well as the specific areas of caution where you will need to be more intentional. For this to be useful, you must be honest with yourself. Only then will you be able to determine the elements that will aid in mastery.

Use the assessment to plot and pinpoint your style. Leadership coaching personalities can be defined by four distinct styles: Analytical Leader, People Leader, Results Leader, and Thought Leader. No one style is better than another, but it is beneficial to identify *your* style to help you determine which qualities or traits will help you be most effective, and which may render you less effective. Understanding this will help you be a better leader coach.

You are most likely a blend of more than one style. Use the following descriptions to plot yourself in the graph to see where your strong leanings are.

Analytical Leader	People Leader
Results Leader	Thought Leader

Analytical Leader

This leader focuses on gathering facts and making decisions based on the available data. *Analytical Leaders* are natural problem solvers who use a logical and practical approach to resolve issues. They are detail oriented and cautious decision makers who use a step-by-step, methodical approach to mitigate risk.

Coaching Strengths: Analytical Leaders are calm, unemotional, and rational in their coaching. This is especially significant for coaching an employee who is indecisive or in an emotionally charged situation. As the leader coach, you excel in guiding them through a step-by-step approach to view the problem analytically and remove the emotion that interferes with objective decision making. This persuades the employee to take a more methodical approach to resolution.

Coaching Cautions: Leaders who fall into this category desire gathering all the details before making a decision. If this describes you, others may view you as a perfectionist who wants more and more data. In your coaching, you will need to know everything about a situation, but may fail to explore the underlying cause of what is stopping the employee from taking action.

Your tendency in coaching is to minimize emotion. As a result, you may miss an opportunity to explore how the employee feels about a situation. This insight can illuminate the best way to coach this employee. Additionally, you may be very good at helping employees weigh pros and cons, but be aware that your conversation with the employee is not a detailed investigation. Rather, it is a means to empower the employee to learn how to weigh their own pros and cons.

Results Leader

This leader has a more directive style that focuses on completion. They are results oriented, decisive, and direct. They appreciate making quick decisions and achieving results. The *Results Leader* has a bias toward action and will be quick to take action themselves if things are not moving fast enough.

Coaching Strengths: Results Leaders are decisive and will keep the employee focused on the outcome or end result they desire. You will embrace the Execution step in the SAGE Coaching Approach. This is especially beneficial when the employee is feeling conflicted or is procrastinating. As the leader coach, you encourage taking swift action from a direct and head-on approach to confront and resolve the problem.

Coaching Cautions: Leaders who fall into this category have a tendency to become impatient if things are not moving fast enough. As a result, you may not invest ample time to progress through the SAGE Coaching Approach. Instead, when the employee is struggling, you will give them the answer to help expedite things. But this only helps them in the short term, as they are not empowered to solve problems long term.

If this describes you, you like being in charge, and your directive style may cause you to give advice when you should be coaching. You may think there is only one way to solve a problem or accomplish a goal. You may stand firm and be inflexible to explore alternatives, especially if it seems that path will take more time.

People Leader

This leader is focused on bringing people together to explore alternatives. They are empathetic, desire harmony, and enjoy making a personal connection. They are tuned in to people's feelings and want to ensure everyone is happy. People Leaders are collaborative, value consensus, and emphasize working together to achieve results.

Coaching Strengths: As a *People Leader* you take a genuine interest in the employee and demonstrate a high level of empathy for where they are laboring. This can be extremely helpful with an employee who lacks confidence. You look upon this as a partnership where collaboration helps them succeed, and you leverage a high amount of encouragement to help them persevere.

Coaching Cautions: Leaders who fall into this category have a tendency to talk more than listen. As a result, you may miss key clues as to why the employee is struggling, clues which will help you successfully progress through the SAGE Coaching Approach.

You can also get emotionally invested in an employee and may not ask the tough questions needed in coaching. If this describes you, your natural tendency is to avoid giving critical feedback that could cause someone to become defensive or uncomfortable. Your need for consensus and harmony may make it difficult for you to coach the employee on a challenging decision, especially if it impacts others negatively.

Thought Leader

This leader focuses on the big picture, likes creative ways to solve problems, and enjoys brainstorming to uncover new alternatives and options. *Thought Leaders* are future oriented and prefer looking at the problem in totality rather than getting bogged down in the specific details in their decision making.

Coaching Strengths: The *Thought Leader* embraces the Alternatives and Options step in the SAGE Coaching Approach. You relish in the opportunity to think outside the box and help the employee explore alternative paths. The employee who is stuck or feels as if they have hit an insurmountable impediment will appreciate your leadership. As the leader coach, you guide the employee to brainstorm various scenarios they had not thought of to solve their setback.

Coaching Cautions: Leaders who fall into this category may miss the clarity needed to help an employee stay grounded and determine key steps to accomplish short-term goals. Since your focus is on the longer-term, strategic view, you may overlook the necessary steps or data to help an employee make a decision and identify the specific actions they need to take today, given all the great ideas you are capable of generating.

If this describes you, you may advocate for more out-of-the-box thinking. This might cause an employee to commit to a course of action you want them to take, but may not be a good fit for them. If the recommended action is not of their own making, you may find accountability plummet. This is where passing the baton to the employee for ownership of the decision is essential.

The Decision Is Yours

To be a great leader coach, you must be self-aware and leverage your strengths while mitigating your challenges. If you want to develop other high-performing leaders, you need to make some changes in your approach.

Now is the time to take action and make a conscious decision to approach your team differently and coach them regularly.

As you learn the SAGE Coaching Approach, keep in mind the strengths and cautions for your style, and how that impacts your ability to develop your team and develop yourself into a great leader coach.

Your Call to Action

Reflections I Will Make

Which leadership style best describes you?

- ☐ Analytical Leader
- ☐ Results Leader
- ☐ People Leader
- ☐ Thought Leader

Actions I Will Take

1. Reflect on which traits describe you the most based on your leadership style. What specific qualities do you demonstrate that are most effective? Make a list referring to the Leader Coach Assessment under the coaching *strengths* that resonate the most.

2. What specific qualities do you demonstrate that are less effective, given your leadership coaching style? Make a list using the coaching *cautions* under the Leader Coach Assessment.

3. With whom can you confirm your assessment? Ask employees on your team for feedback on your style to validate your strengths and cautions. As you learn more about the SAGE Coaching Approach, think about your style and where you can leverage your strengths and how to mitigate areas for development around each area of caution.

Go to www.thesagealliance.com/worksheets to download the following worksheet that will help you plot your leader coach style.

sage
alliance

Leader Coach Assessment

Check all the boxes that describe you. Be honest with your answers to get an appreciation for your leader coaching style.

Analytical Leader	People Leader
Strengths	**Strengths**
❑ Natural problem solver	❑ Empathetic, tuned in to feelings
❑ Fact-based decisions	❑ Brings people together
❑ Logical, methodical, and practical	❑ Supportive, encouraging, and empathetic
❑ Calm, objective, and rational	❑ Collaborative, consensus driven
Cautions	**Cautions**
❑ Perfectionist	❑ Overly emotionally invested
❑ Needs more data	❑ Talks more than listens
❑ Fails to explore underlying cause	❑ Avoids giving critical feedback
❑ Overlooks employee feelings	❑ Bypasses tough decisions
Strengths	**Strengths**
❑ Driven to achieve results	❑ Big picture, future oriented
❑ Decisive and focused on the outcome	❑ Naturally creative problem solver
❑ Encourages swift action	❑ Enjoys brainstorming
❑ Direct, confronts problems head on	❑ Thinks outside the box
Cautions	**Cautions**
❑ Impatient	❑ Misses out on clarity
❑ Takes charge of situations	❑ Overlooks key steps or data
❑ Dispenses advice/instructions	❑ Neglects clarity on specific actions
❑ Stands firm, inflexible	❑ Avoids giving decision authority
Results Leader	Thought Leader

What qualities do you demonstrate that are most effective for your leader coach style?

_____

_____

What qualities do you demonstrate that are least effective for your leader coach style?

_____

_____

© Sage Alliance 2019   www.thesagealliance.com

The SAGE
Coaching Approach

It's Time to Coach

Through the SAGE Coaching Approach, you become the sounding board who encourages employees to take on new challenges, explore different perspectives, and solve critical problems. Employees feel empowered and have the authority to make the critical decisions to reach a successful outcome.

Coaching takes time. Unfortunately, leaders have little time to spend with their employees who are already stretched beyond their means and are struggling with disparate priorities and the plethora of demands placed upon them. And as you focus on action and results, it becomes increasingly more challenging to carve out the needed time to coach your team, especially with imminent deadlines. But you must make the time. Otherwise you create an environment of dependency, and you hinder the advancement of your employees, the outcomes for your organization, and the progression of your own leadership development.

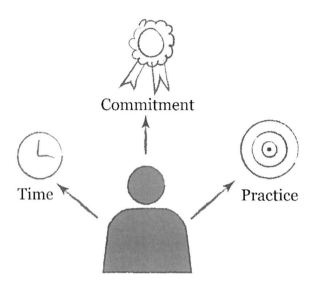

Coaching takes commitment—yours. It requires *you* to make the commitment and to remain accountable to that commitment. To remain committed, you must be intentional about coaching. The SAGE Coaching Approach will empower you to instill confidence in your team to make tough decisions.

Coaching takes practice, just like mastering any new skill. Use every interaction with your team to coach. The more you do this, the more this will become second nature, and the more comfortable and competent you will become. Later in this chapter, we will look at a repeatable process through the SAGE Coaching Approach that will help you become a master leader coach.

Every great leader coach understands it takes an investment of time, commitment, and practice. When you choose to manage these three variables, you will find numerous opportunities to coach. So you must ask yourself these critical questions: Am I leading in the way I want? Am I investing the time to coach now? What indicates that my leadership style includes a coaching approach?

There Is a Better Way

As you saw in chapter 1, *you think you're coaching, but you're not!* Most leaders I work with tell me they coach their employees frequently, and even pride themselves on being great coaches. However, when I dig deeper, I discover they are not coaching. Although they are supportive, have an open-door policy, and listen to their direct reports, they are advising and directing the outcome instead of coaching. Most importantly, they are not getting the results they expect from their team, they are unable to identify what needs to change, and therefore, they are undermining their own success, the productivity of their team, and the bottom line of their organization.

If you're uncertain as to whether your current leadership approach is actually coaching, explore the scenario of Ethan and his manager, Sara, whom we met in chapter 2.

You Think You're Coaching: Sara and Ethan

How many Mondays can there be in one week? Ethan thinks to himself. Ever since he kicked off this latest initiative, which has an extremely tight deadline, he has felt overwhelmed. His team already has three initiatives behind schedule, and he's beginning to feel the pressure from other departments.

The team is being asked to think more strategically, despite multiple responsibilities and overlapping deadlines, for each of the initiatives. Whenever Ethan gets ahead, he loses traction and falls behind. With all the priorities and requests for his time during the workday, he finds it easier to stay late and work on the weekends to get everything done instead of spending the extra time to coach his team. He figures this is the price he has to pay to be part of the leadership team.

Ethan doesn't see any way to get ahead, and he's starting to feel that the promotion he desperately wants is getting further out of reach. Seeing no clear solution, he approaches his manager, Sara, for advice, as he often does.

"Hey Sara, do you have a minute?" he asks sheepishly as he peers through the door Sara keeps cracked as a sign of her "open-door policy."

Sara looks up from her laptop. She's been crunching numbers all day to finalize next year's budget plan. With a forced smile and a deep sigh, she motions for Ethan to take a seat. As soon as he does, he explains the situation. In a distraught tone, he explains that he is at a crossroads as to how to complete all his work in a timely fashion while helping the team innovate so they can capitalize on future opportunities.

Ethan has taken this seat several times in the last six months to share his feelings of having too much on his plate and to gain direction for how to solve his predicament. Having been with the company for four years, he has expressed his aspirations in assuming greater responsibilities, managing a larger team, and taking his career forward to the next step. Sara has shared with him her concerns that he must learn how to delegate more effectively if he wants to be promoted. She knows he is a self-starter, but unfortunately, he struggles to get everything done.

"Ethan, you know I get it. I've been where you are," Sara says.

He knows she understands his situation. After all, Sara worked her way up from middle management. Because of that experience, he knows she has the perfect solution for him.

"Your team is taking on more than usual, and that's tough for everyone," Sara continues. "It's going to be impossible for you to get everything done if you don't delegate some of your tasks and collaborate with the other departments on deadlines. You and your team need to be thinking about the strategic implications as well."

This is perfectly sound advice, as far as Ethan is concerned. He wishes he were a better delegator, but he doesn't know where to begin, and he feels uncomfortable delegating more work to his already overwhelmed team.

"Here's what you need to do," Sara says. "Take the top two high-priority initiatives and hold on to them. Then, meet with each of your team members and discuss who can take on each of the remaining tasks. This way they will feel they had a say in things."

"I knew you would know what to do!" Ethan is ecstatic. Sara always gives him the best advice, and that's why he comes straight to her whenever he runs into a problem. Sara has always been a supportive manager, willing to listen. Ethan feels comfortable reaching out for her advice and then following her instructions.

If you think this is coaching, think again! The above scenario puts Sara (the manager) front and center in solving Ethan's (the employee) issues. With this approach, Ethan will constantly rely on Sara to solve his challenges. There is a better way.

The SAGE Coaching Approach

As you learned in the previous chapter, becoming an effective leader who grooms your team to develop their own leadership skills requires you to adopt a leader coach approach. Here, the focus is on empowering your employees to think for themselves and solve problems on their own, with you as the leader coach, facilitating the conversation.

That is exactly what the SAGE Coaching Approach achieves. You become the sounding board who encourages employees to take on new challenges, explore different perspectives, and solve critical problems. Employees feel empowered and have the authority to make the critical decisions to reach a successful outcome. And you do this through an interactive approach of asking questions, listening, and being observant, which leads to uncovering the root cause of the issues and challenges.

Armed with this knowledge, you can facilitate a brainstorming session where you guide employees to explore alternatives and options and offer different perspectives to their business challenge. This gives them the tools to be decisive, commit to a course of action, and be accountable for those actions.

Learning how to implement this coaching approach is as easy as 1-2-3. Well, maybe 1-2-3-4, since there are four comprehensive steps in the SAGE Coaching Approach:

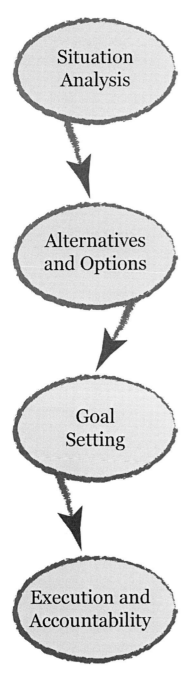

S: Situation Analysis
A: Alternatives and Options
G: Goal Setting
E: Execution and Accountability

Situation Analysis

Focus on understanding the situation from the employee's perspective. It's not about collecting all the data involving a particular situation, but rather identifying the employee's challenges and the obstacles standing in *their* way. This sets the foundation for this coaching approach. Without clarifying the issues facing the employee, you cannot be an effective leader coach.

Alternatives and Options

Brainstorm options together to help the employee generate alternatives, along with expected outcomes. There typically is more than one option for solving a problem. Once you have uncovered several options, discuss and weigh the pros and cons for each before inspiring the employee to choose the best one. This step will help you empower your team to think on their own and be decisive, with you as the facilitator, not the problem solver.

Goal Setting

Set goals together and gain clarity on those goals. This motivates employees, ensures everyone is on the same page, and encourages them to achieve their goals in a timely fashion. Ultimately, you are galvanizing the employee to define the key goals and the associated steps to address the challenges that were identified during Situation Analysis.

Execution and Accountability

Establish ownership and accountability to ensure successful execution. Without this, the employee may not be fully committed to take action, which will impede moving initiatives forward. When you encourage and empower an employee to take ownership of a role, and then agree on their accountability for completing the task, they are motivated to take action. Encouragement is an important part of this step. Expectations are clear, measurements are formalized, and timing is identified so the employee will be successful.

In the following chapters, we will explore how to implement the SAGE Coaching Approach in more detail, along with exercises and tips that will help you transform from manager to leader coach.

Go to www.thesagealliance.com/worksheets for a worksheet with questions to ask at each stage.

Your Call to Action

Reflections I Will Make

Rate the areas you would like to improve based on where you see yourself *now*. Be honest and reflect where you excel and where you can improve in each of the SAGE Coaching Approach steps. Use a scale of 1–5: (5) **Excellent,** (4) **Good,** (3) **Average,** (2) **Fair,** (1) **Poor.**

- ☐ Situation Analysis
  - ○ Clarify the challenges and obstacles
  - ○ Ask questions to uncover the root cause
  - ○ Listen and be curious
- ☐ Alternatives and Options
  - ○ Brainstorm options
  - ○ Weigh pros and cons
  - ○ Encourage choosing the most advantageous option
- ☐ Goal Setting
  - ○ Clarify goals
  - ○ Gain alignment around goals and actions
  - ○ Help make goals actionable
- ☐ Execution and Accountability
  - ○ Establish ownership
  - ○ Build accountability
  - ○ Provide encouragement and motivation

Actions I Will Take

1. What are some immediate opportunities for you to coach? Think of a recent scenario with one or two of your direct reports. Walk through how you will empower each of them using the SAGE Coaching Approach. What do you see as the specific challenge(s) for you in each step? How will you remain accountable to invest the time to coach, e.g. identify an accountability partner, create daily reminders, schedule one-on-ones, etc.

2. As you think about adopting the SAGE Coaching Approach, what is most effective about your leader coach style (Analytical, Results, People, Thought) that will help you make this transformation?

3. What do you see as least effective about your leader coach style (Analytical, Results, People, Thought) for

you to move from good to great in implementing the SAGE Coaching Approach?

Go to www.thesagealliance.com/worksheets to download the following worksheet that will help you chart your progress.

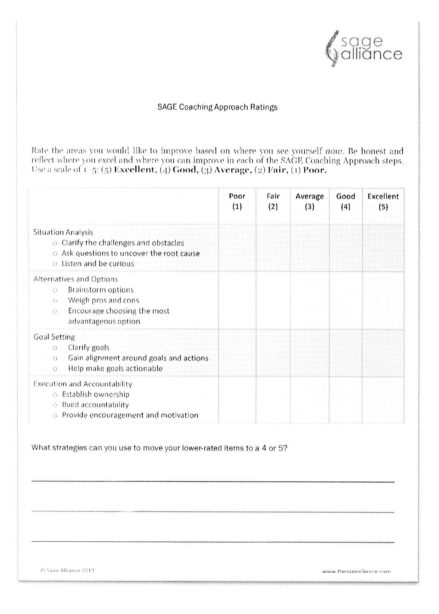

Situation Analysis: Get Curious

Ask open-ended questions to uncover what is really happening below the surface. This requires you to stay focused on the context instead of the details and inevitably jumping into solution mode.

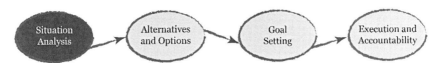

Offering advice, solving a problem, and resolving conflict are great behaviors if you want to be viewed as the hero among your team. You are presented with a problem and you immediately have the answer. Great. But are you prepared to always be available and have the answer to every challenge?

You Think You're Coaching: Ethan's Story

Ethan is overwhelmed. It seems whenever he starts to get ahead on his projects, he loses traction and falls behind. He does not have the time to teach his team the nuances associated with all the initiatives he manages. With looming deadlines and lots of requests for his time, he has found it easier to stay late and work on the weekends to get everything done. He thinks of this as the price he must pay to be part of the leadership team. It's been four years and Ethan aspires to taking on greater responsibilities and managing a larger team.

Sara sees Ethan as a self-starter and someone with high potential on her team but also notes he struggles with getting everything done. In their one-on-one, Sara shares her concerns that he needs to delegate more effectively if he wants to be promoted.

"Ethan, I agree that we have some big initiatives with tight deadlines," she says. "It's impossible for you to get everything done if you don't delegate some of your projects. Your team has to take on more. I know it's hard, but there is no other option."

Ethan hesitates. He has some concerns about delegating, but does not want to disappoint Sara.

Can you identify why this isn't the best approach for Sara to help Ethan?

Awaken Your Curiosity

Sara has a team of one hundred people, with ten employees reporting directly to her. Is it possible, or even smart, that she always has the solution to every challenge they face? If each of her direct reports comes to her each time they face a challenge, she would spend her entire day putting out fires rather than leading her team.

As a leader coach, you (and Sara) adopt the SAGE Coaching Approach and not only gain back time in your day, but you also practice effective leadership skills that empower your team to solve challenges, and demonstrate to them how they can lead their own teams. It all begins by practicing a simple characteristic you've embodied all your life: curiosity.

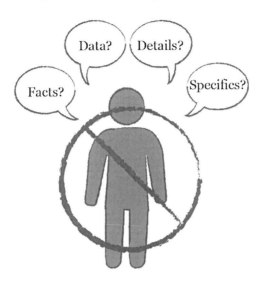

When approached by an employee facing a challenge, analyzing the situation is the first place a good leader coach will start. But here's the twist. Instead of focusing on uncovering an exhaustive array of facts, data, and details, Situation Analysis looks at the obstacles and challenges *from the employee's perspective.* The focus is not on the details, but on the employee's perception and understanding of their challenges. Therefore, you must enter the Situation Analysis phase of the SAGE Coaching Approach with curiosity and an open mind. Leveraging the power of your curiosity helps you understand what the employee is encountering or struggling with, and helps the employee grasp the root cause of their challenge.

By asking open-ended, thought-provoking questions, two critical opportunities unfold:

1. You gain the needed insights to successfully coach the employee.
2. The employee gains clarity on how they can develop the solution themselves.

Your purpose is to help the employee clarify the key challenges, obstacles, and specific problems standing in the way of their goal.

At the start of the conversation, you may want to know all the facts. After all, you are a great problem solver and data gatherer, and as such you want to solve the problem for your employee. When you see someone struggling in a specific area, your instinct is to help them. Therefore, you go immediately into solution mode.

As you saw earlier in the chapter, Sara too went into problem-solving mode by offering her top-notch, expert advice. And Ethan appreciated her insight. This is not to say there aren't times you may need to provide your expertise; however, this is not coaching. Your peremptory advice will not empower employees to learn how to solve problems on their own.

One caution is to be aware of occasions when you are preoccupied or constricted by time. You feel rushed, and an employee's challenge feels more like an interruption than an opportunity to practice your leader coach skills and develop theirs. This is when it becomes easier to dispense advice, instead of coach, so you can get back to your mounting workload.

A more effective approach is to get curious about the situation the employee is facing. Ask open-ended questions to uncover what is really happening below the surface. This requires you to stay focused on the context instead of the details and inevitably jumping into solution mode. Take the time to explore not only *what* is happening but *why*.

Get to the Root Cause

In the example, Ethan is struggling with delegating. Sara has a rudimentary grasp of what is happening, but she has not uncovered the core of why the problem exists (Ethan's aversion to delegating). Why is Ethan struggling and why is he seeking Sara's advice in the first place? Is it because he fears losing control? Does he not trust his team to follow through and carry out the task? Perhaps he feels some of his employees need additional training before he can delegate.

All too often, the problem the employee presents is not really the problem at all. Just like an iceberg, which has a visible section above the waterline and a larger, invisible section below the waterline, an employee's problem is much the same. What you observe is only the tip of the iceberg. The underlying root cause is below the surface. Your role as a leader coach is to look deeper, below the surface, to uncover what is really going on. This is how you help the employee get to the root cause.

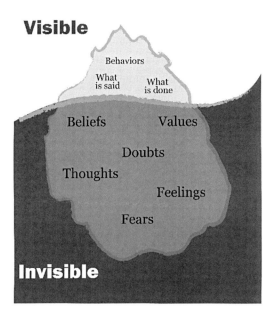

Ask open-ended, thought-provoking questions and listen for the clues that indicate the root cause of the employee's challenge. These questions should enlighten you as to any underlying fears, doubts, or beliefs and should cause the employee to realize critical areas he or she may have overlooked. Sample questions are at the end of this chapter.

Let's look at how Sara could use Situation Analysis to uncover the root cause with Ethan and his challenge with delegating.

Rewind: What's beneath the Surface?

Sara recognizes delegation is a challenge for Ethan. He and his team have taken on several high-profile initiatives over the past year, and she feels the pressure of the deadlines just as he does. But she knows that for her entire team to earn the recognition and advancement they deserve, they have to work together. As their leader coach, she must help them meet the challenges head on, develop innovative solutions, and produce results.

As a high-potential leader in his own right, Ethan must step up to the plate. Sara knows he is capable of doing so. Ethan seems willing to look at different ways to better manage his workload and his team. But Sara knows that if he constantly relies on her for answers, he will never earn the respect he needs from his team, nor develop the skills and confidence needed to be a great leader.

Sara knows Ethan is open to her advice, but she feels he is not steadfast to solve the problems himself. She decides to apply the SAGE Coaching Approach she has learned and wants her direct reports to adopt.

As she analyzes the situation with Ethan, Sara determines she needs to uncover what is really standing in the way of his success.

"Ethan, I agree that we have some big initiatives

with tight deadlines," she says. "What are you struggling with the most right now?"

As Ethan recites a litany of challenges, Sara takes mental note of the words and phrases he uses. It is clear his issue lies primarily with delegation. Although Sara wants to help Ethan be a better delegator, she needs to uncover what is at the core of this issue. If she doesn't, Ethan will be back in her office for additional advice when he gets overwhelmed again.

Through a series of questions, Sara allows Ethan the opportunity to share what is causing him to avoid delegating. The answers provide them both greater insight into the root cause of his challenge.

"So, where do you need help?" she asks.

Ethan pauses to consider Sara's question. She can sense he has been so laser focused on the problem that he has not yet considered where he needs help. After some thought, Ethan explains he doesn't trust others to do their jobs, so he ends up micromanaging them.

Sara poses a follow-up question. "What have you tried so far, Ethan?"

Ethan lists the actions he has taken, and admits he has not been consistent in delegating to his team. From what Sara can tell, he hesitates to delegate for fear he will not know what is going on if Sara or one of the other executives asks him about his team's progress. Listening patiently, Sara nods and assures Ethan they can work together to come up with a solution.

Ethan's aversion to delegating *seems* like the issue. But with further questioning, Sara realizes the real issue is his fear of losing control. She concludes that the situation with Ethan is threefold:

1. He doesn't trust others to do their work as well as he could; essentially, he's micromanaging.
2. He has no clear process for his team to report their progress to him.
3. He is concerned about looking foolish and tarnishing his reputation with his superiors.

She arrives at this conclusion through the practice of listening actively and demonstrating curiosity through asking thought-provoking questions, which are foundational principles in the Situation Analysis step of the SAGE Coaching Approach.

Who, What, Where, and How?

Before you can attempt to solve the problem, you must probe for the challenge or issue. Essentially, get curious. Don't assume you know why an employee is plagued with a particular challenge. Ask the employee thought-provoking questions to trigger where they are struggling and provide insight into the core issue.

Explore what is going on with the employee, the obstacles standing in their way, and the challenges they are facing. Do not rush into solution mode at this point. Instead, invest time exploring their current reality from their perspective before moving to the next step.

Becoming curious means asking questions to ensure you understand your employee's challenges. This approach helps you get to the root cause—the why behind the challenge. Analyzing the situation using curiosity also helps you avoid projecting your own past experiences, challenges, or solutions onto the employee you are coaching. After all, the solution you reached in a similar situation might not apply to this employee and their challenge.

Offering solutions comes naturally for you because you want to help someone younger or less experienced in their career than you. The drawback with this is it takes the form of mentoring or advising, which is not coaching. Coaching is a powerful way to ensure maximum engagement and empowerment.

Practice asking open-ended questions, and guard against offering the solution. Stay away from close-ended questions, ones that start with *would you* as in *Would you like help?* The only response is yes or no, which doesn't illuminate the area of challenge and will lead to you offering a solution. Questions that start with *Who*, *What*, *Where*, and *How* elicit valuable information regarding the situation and lay the foundation to coach.

Successful coaching happens when you take a bird's-eye view of the situation and ask questions to help employees explore a challenge more deeply for themselves.

What questions can you ask to understand the situation and guide employees toward greater insight for themselves? Here are some examples:

- What is the current situation?

- ⁓ What is your assessment of what's going on?
- ⁓ What do you make of all this?
- ⁓ What feedback would be helpful for you to gain on this situation?
- ⁓ Where do you need help?
- ⁓ What are you struggling with the most right now?
- ⁓ What is getting in the way of success?
- ⁓ What will you gain by mastering this skill?
- ⁓ What obstacles are standing in your way?
- ⁓ What is stopping you from making this decision?
- ⁓ What have you already tried? What is the impact of this?
- ⁓ Who have you spoken to about the situation?
- ⁓ How do you want it to be if all goes as planned?

Visit www.thesagealliance.com/worksheets for a list of questions that will assist you at this stage in the coaching process.

Your Call to Action

Reflections I Will Make

- ☐ Ask more *who* questions
- ☐ Ask more *what* questions
- ☐ Ask more *where* questions
- ☐ Ask more *how* questions

Actions I Will Take

What open-ended questions can help you empower your team and improve as a leader coach? Make a list. While you will adjust your questions for different situations, this list will get you started.

1. Schedule a one-on-one with a direct report who is struggling with a challenge or obstacle. In this meeting, ask the employee no fewer than five questions

that will offer you more insight into where *they* are struggling. When you and the employee believe you have identified the root cause—and only then—you can begin to talk about next steps. Through this practice, you will begin to train yourself to ask open-ended questions before offering solutions.

2. Practice curiosity in a meeting with your team to discuss an area where they are facing a challenge, but have not yet come up with a resolution. Your goal is to ask as many open-ended questions as you can. When employees ask you a question, before answering, pause and think through the impetus for their question. Discern the motivation behind the question and what the employee is seeking to understand. Then, practice asking more questions to get to the root cause and uncover meaningful information on the issue your team is facing. You are not solving the problem, but uncovering the challenges that stand in the way of your team solving the problem on their own.

3. How will your leader coach style (Analytical, Results, People, Thought) help you master uncovering the root cause? What are the cautions that will get in the way of you being effective? Identify situations where you are predisposed to a particular solution or approach. How will you remain curious and be open? What will you do to shift your perspective when you have a strong belief about the right way to solve a problem? Make a list of strategies you can implement to stay on track and questions you can ask to uncover the root cause.

Go to www.thesagealliance.com/worksheets to download the following worksheet to help you chart your progress.

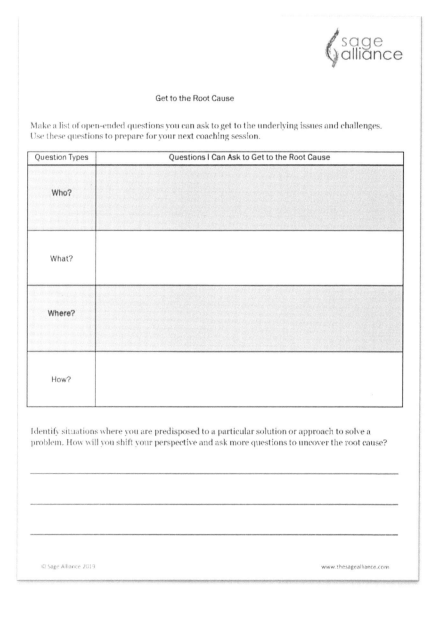

Alternatives and Options: The Good, the Bad, and the Shades in between

Employees learn how to analyze options and distinguish a good option from a not-so-good option by looking at the problem from different perspectives. You are the catalyst for helping employees develop critical-thinking skills to uncover and address alternatives, and collaboratively explore what could work versus what will not work.

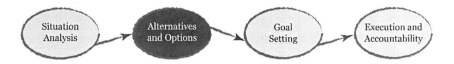

With all the complexity and uncertainty your employees face, implementing the SAGE Coaching Approach helps them look at a situation from different perspectives, explore options, weigh pros and cons, and feel confident taking initiative and being decisive. When you become proficient with the SAGE Coaching Approach, you are modeling a leader coach and demonstrating to your team one of the most effective approaches to leadership. They appreciate the investment you make in their growth and development.

You Think You're Coaching: Sara and Ethan

Sara is swamped with her own deadlines. Things have

heated up in recent months, but she knows she needs to help Ethan before he crashes and burns. She has helped Ethan uncover his genuine challenge with delegating, which is his fear of losing control.

Sara begins, "Ethan, why don't you select some lower-profile projects and have the employees on your team shadow you to learn the ropes?"

Ethan is pleased with Sara's advice. He nods his agreement, thinking Sara always knows how to help. He decides to act on her advice and sit down with his team to identify the low-hanging fruit, have his team members accompany him to meetings, and begin delegating those projects.

You should have noticed Sara was preoccupied with her own deadlines, and while she provided her expert advice, she was not coaching or empowering Ethan to think for himself. There are times you may need to provide expert advice, but this is not coaching, and this will not empower Ethan to solve the problem on his own in the future.

They Need to Think for Themselves

Think of an employee who continually comes to you whenever they hit a roadblock, just like Ethan. When more than one employee does this, you become the problem solver for all the issues your team faces, whether large or small.

As the manager, you want to help your team overcome challenges and obstacles. However, when you provide the solution, time and time again, this trains them to come back the next time they face a challenge instead of figuring it out on their own. They begin to expect your assistance every time they hit a roadblock. This becomes a vicious cycle. It's not practical for you to be the problem solver on a regular basis, and doing so prevents employees from learning how to solve problems on their own.

Instead, as the leader coach, you want to empower employees to think for themselves, build their capabilities, and grow their confidence. You hire, train, and manage smart people. Now, as a leader coach, you help them develop the confidence to solve their work-related issues, and simultaneously develop into great leaders themselves. In more instances than not, your employees know the solution to their issue. Often, they worry about making the wrong decision and therefore don't take the risk.

These feelings ensue from extrinsic motivation, i.e. the Carrot-and-Stick Approach. This was derived from the old story that you offer a carrot to a donkey as a means to entice him to move and pull his cart forward. In contrast, if he refuses, he receives a jab from behind as punishment for not moving. This approach has long been proven to be ineffective. In the long term, this creates an environment where employees feel apprehensive, indecisive, and/or powerless. They worry that they will fail or look foolish.

Instead, you need to drive results through intrinsic motivation: the sheer satisfaction of a job well done (by the employee). When they learn and master a new skill, and accomplish this autonomously, they are more energized, take ownership, and look for opportunities to go the extra mile. How do you create this environment?

Employees learn how to analyze options and distinguish a good option from a not-so-good option by looking at the problem from different perspectives. You are the catalyst for helping employees develop critical-thinking skills to uncover and address alternatives, and collaboratively explore what could work versus what will not work. You help them in three ways:

1. Learn a repeatable process to think through and assess issues they encounter, both now and in the future.
2. Gain confidence in their ability to make decisions, even those fraught with complexity.
3. Rely on their own instincts and creative problem-solving skills before seeking out your counsel.

Let's see how Sara models this step in the SAGE Coaching Approach.

Rewind: That's One Option, What's Another?

Sara has helped Ethan uncover his genuine challenge with delegating, which is his fear of losing control. She knows what obstacles stand in his way: the ability to let go of work and trust his team, and concern for his reputation with those in senior management. With this information, she works with Ethan to explore Alternatives and Options to improve his delegation skills, gain the needed trust in his employees, and improve his leadership effectiveness.

"So, Ethan, it sounds like fear of losing control is the real issue here. What do you think can be done to help you feel more comfortable delegating tasks to your team?"

Ethan suggests a few ideas—identifying lower-visibility tasks, assigning team members to stretch goals, or hiring a new employee to fill the open role. Sara can see a hint of satisfaction in Ethan as he explores these alternatives. She knows this is difficult for him, but she believes he is capable of reaching an advantageous solution to his delegating dilemma.

"These sound like good ideas," she says. "How do you want to stay informed in regard to your team's progress so you feel more comfortable delegating?"

This question gets Ethan thinking. "Well, last year we implemented biweekly one-on-one meetings, but we haven't followed through with them. Maybe we could reinstitute those." Now Ethan is thinking for himself, rather than relying on Sara for the answer. "I could create a schedule where each of the four teams reports to me weekly, on a rotating basis," he continues. "This way I'll know what's happening week by week without having to hunt down people to pull information from them."

"Sounds great!" Sara encourages. "That's one option. What are some others?"

She listens as Ethan explores other ideas to help him remain in the loop with his team and each of their initiatives. He can use these ideas to delegate and feel content everyone is performing at their best. With that, he will feel more comfortable when questioned by anyone from senior management, and he will be more equipped to suggest his point of view when needed.

After listening to Ethan share options for addressing each underlying issue, Sara takes a unique approach. Instead of suggesting which option Ethan should choose, she asks him, "What is the craziest thing you could do?"

Ethan grins. "I could delegate all of my work."

Sara does not hesitate with her response and confirms this is certainly an option to explore. As good as it sounds, both she and Ethan know this is unrealistic, and they agree to explore additional options. Finally, through brainstorming they arrive at several viable options, each of which helps Ethan address the issues he's facing related to delegating.

Sara then asks Ethan what he sees as the pros and cons of each option. Ethan examines each separately, with Sara as a sounding board. She suggests he rank the options for feasibility. He has the start of a plan and can begin to get a handle on things.

But Sara has one more question for Ethan. "What would happen if you did nothing?"

Perplexed, Ethan takes a moment before replying, "Doing nothing isn't an option, not if I want to continue feeling inundated with work, and not if I ever want to get promoted. I need to move some of this work to my team to allow them to develop their skills, so I can focus my time on setting the strategic direction."

You Are Not the Problem Solver

When you practice this approach, employees are empowered to come up with options on their own. The purpose is not to find the *right* approach, but rather to brainstorm thought-provoking questions to gain a new perspective.

Only after all options have been exhausted should you weigh

the pros and cons of efficacy. If you stop when you think you have uncovered the solution, you are not helping the employee evaluate the risks and ramifications for their actions. Developing these skills positions employees to solve problems and determine the best approach independently, both now and in the future.

The SAGE Coaching Approach inherently helps employees distinguish between various alternatives and become resolute to a course of action. This helps teach them how to solve not only today's challenges but future challenges. As the leader coach, you are the catalyst for helping to bring the array of options to the forefront and not narrowly focusing on solving the immediate challenge.

You know what your team needs to do to accomplish their goals. When a challenge arises, you want them to arrive at the best solution given the circumstances. You want them to solve the problem themselves. You are not the problem solver. You know they can do it; you just have to get out of the way.

Allowing your team to solve the problem themselves accomplishes four objectives:

1. They feel more **confident** in their ability to solve problems.
2. They feel **empowered** to make tough decisions after a process of critical thinking.
3. They take **ownership** of their solutions and the outcomes.
4. They see your **investment** (of time and support) as a leader coach who believes in their abilities.

When an employee asks what you think they should do, that is your opportunity to turn the question around by asking, "What do *you* think you should do?" They already know the answer—or, at least, have some ideas—but they do not have the *confidence* to make the decision on their own.

Exploring alternatives and options helps them make tough decisions, and to do it with confidence. As a leader coach, you *empower* your employees to think for themselves and trust they have the authority to make critical decisions. In most cases, there is more than one option for solving a problem. While one solution may be more efficient or take less time, there are a variety of ways to reach a desired outcome. Empowered employees think for themselves, make the tough calls, and are decisive, even in the presence of complexity and uncertainty.

Exploring alternatives and options accelerates *ownership* by helping employees learn how to trust their instincts. *Ownership* is not particularly high when you tell employees what to do. In this instance, you (not they) own the decision and the outcome. This is ineffective in grooming future leaders, and your employees will continue to depend on you to solve their problems.

When you delegate authority, your employees realize they are responsible for the outcome and that you trust their judgment. This may include having them rank the options, from highest to lowest probability of success, to determine the best solution, and anticipating potential problems and reflecting on accompanying solutions. As a result, employees have the staying power to take charge and see a decision through, regardless of the bumps in the road, and remain accountable for their decisions.

When employees see you press the pause button from the pressures of your everyday workload to coach, they feel more connected to you as the leader. Your investment of your time and belief in their abilities helps boost confidence and engagement, and they will continue to strive to do more.

As the leader coach, not the problem solver, you provide a safe forum for them to discuss the issue and weigh the pros and cons for each option before choosing the best course of action. Now you are using the SAGE Coaching Approach. When you master this step, you will be amazed when one of your employees comes into your office and says, "I know what you're going to ask me. You're going to ask me what options I've thought of and what the associated pros and cons are for each one." Then you will know you have expertly demonstrated this step in the SAGE Coaching Approach.

Sara leveraged the SAGE Coaching Approach in several areas:

Sara asked thought-provoking questions to help Ethan explore and uncover several options. An example includes "What if you did nothing?" When Ethan realized doing nothing is not an option, he volunteered other alternatives. When Sara asked, "Then what can you do?", she allowed Ethan to come up with more options to solve the problem at hand, further challenging him to explore and decide on a specific course of action.

Sara prompted him to weigh the pros and cons of each of the options and rank them based on priority. She also helped him explore alternatives, not only for delegating, but for feeling comfortable while delegating. This showed Ethan how to make better decisions, especially in the face of complexity and uncertainty.

Sara listened, stayed focused, and spent the needed time with Ethan to explore his challenge with delegation. She also helped him feel comfortable with delegating. Had they immediately skipped to the solution, Ethan may not have been fully committed to making the needed changes. This exploration helped Ethan understand the ramifications for taking action versus not taking action, and the shades in between.

It's Not about Finding the Answer

There are four elements for effectively assisting employees to generate sound alternatives and options:

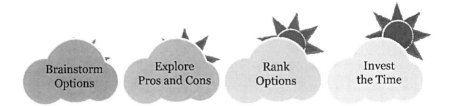

1. Create a list of as many alternative courses of action as possible. The purpose is not to find *the* answer but to generate options. Sara and Ethan did find the answer, but the focus was on generating some viable options through their continued brainstorming. Think of this as a free-form exploration and sharing of ideas. Oftentimes, a better alternative will present itself, but it may take time to get there.

At this stage, you help your employee develop as many options as possible to uncover different courses of action and the consequences of taking one action over another. Through brainstorming, you are not only coaching the employee to solve today's problem, but you are empowering them to solve tomorrow's problems as well.

2. Explore pros and cons of each option. Once you have discussed several options, help them determine which ones make sense, given the specific situation. Without a clear idea of what will and will not work, the employee will hesitate taking action. This alone will help the employee make better decisions *now* as they explore possible solutions to potential problems, and in the future to take ownership of the decision moving forward.

When you make the decision, or tell the employee what to do, you retain ownership. This continues the employee's reliance on you and prevents them from developing in their role.

3. Rank options. This can help when there is no clear best option. Ranking helps you compare each option based on the identified areas of importance. It also enables the employee to identify which option will work well in the short term, and which will work in the long term. Many times, there will be a different option for each one. When this is clear, the employee will feel more confident in choosing a less desirable option if they know they can address any challenges with a long-term solution down the road.

4. Invest the time. Spend the necessary time brainstorming options before moving into solution mode. It takes practice to not immediately volunteer a solution, since you are wired to do just that. But don't settle for quick fixes, and avoid offering a solution. Instead, ask questions when an employee reaches a stumbling block and needs your help. This helps them solve tomorrow's challenges today by equipping them with critical-thinking skills. You are helping them with a well-thought-out plan for how to solve not just the challenges they are currently facing, but those challenges that may present themselves tomorrow.

Here are some questions you can ask at this stage:

- What have you thought about or already tried?
- What do you think could work here?
- What are some options?
- What is the value of brainstorming some options together?
- What else can you do?
- What other options can you think of?
- What could you do differently?
- What is the craziest thing you could do?
- What would happen if you do nothing?
- What would help you feel more comfortable?
- What needs to be in place for you to be successful?
- That's one option, what's another?
- What are the pros and cons (of each option)?
- How do you want to prioritize these options?
- How do you want to rank these options?
- What option do you recommend?

Visit www.thesagealliance.com/worksheets for a list of questions that will assist you at this stage in the coaching process.

Your Call to Action

Reflections I Will Make

Which areas do you want to improve? Check as many as apply.

- ☐ Spend more time brainstorming alternatives and options
- ☐ Generate more than three options
- ☐ Weigh pros and cons
- ☐ Rank each option

Actions I Will Take

1. Think through scenarios where you offered advice to someone on your team to solve a challenge they were facing. What strategies do you want to implement to empower them to think for themselves in the future?

2. Work with employees on your team to help them generate alternatives and options over the ensuing weeks. Generate a minimum of three options in each interaction; however, don't limit yourself. Once you have brainstormed options, only then should you work with the employee to choose a course of action. Set a goal to come up with a minimum of three options, and as many as five, in each coaching situation. See the link at the end of this chapter for a worksheet to facilitate your discussions.

3. Think of each employee on your team. What needs to be in place for you to delegate authority and transfer ownership of the initiative to each of them? How will your leader coach style (Analytical, Results, People, Thought) hinder your ability to be successful?

How can you leverage the strengths of your style to be successful here? What strategies can you implement to stay on track? When will you get started?

Go to www.thesagealliance.com/worksheets to download the following worksheet that will help you chart your progress.

sage
alliance

Brainstorming Alternatives and Options

Step 1: Create a list of as many alternatives courses of action as possible.
Generate options through a free-form brainstorming session.

Step 2: Explore pros and cons of each option.
Identify the positive and potential negative rationale for moving forward with each alternative.

Step 3: Rank options.
Compare options and determine their rank based on where the positive outweighs the negative.

Options	Pros	Cons	Ranked Options
1.			
2.			
3.			
4.			
5.			

www.thesagealliance.com

Goal Setting: Keep on Track

It is critical to help the employee set goals, identify the outcome and its associated steps, and determine how success will be measured in the targeted area. Without this, focus diminishes, motivation wanes, and the path to their goal becomes unclear.

If you're like most people, goal setting often takes the form of New Year's resolutions at the start of the year. You list a few items you would like to accomplish, then put your list away, glance at it from time to time throughout the year, and review it with disappointment in December when you realize you've accomplished a mere percentage of what you set out to do.

Despite the overwhelming body of research that supports the importance of goal setting, only a small percentage of leaders consistently set clearly defined goals for their team. As an executive coach, I am fervent about goal setting and laying out the specific steps needed to reach a goal. When my clients are passionate about reaching their goals, and are committed to remaining accountable, they achieve amazing results.

You Think You're Coaching: Sara and Ethan

Having explored a variety of alternatives, Ethan tells Sara

which option he believes is most ideal to pursue. As Sara nods in agreement, he feels confident that he can work with his team to make it happen.

Sara feels Ethan has a good grasp of what needs to be done, and she needs to run to her next meeting.

"Ethan, I'm thrilled to see you're willing to take immediate action. I look forward to hearing about your progress in our next one-on-one in two weeks."

Ethan agrees, and they both run off to their respective meetings.

What could Sara do differently to ensure Ethan's success?

Set Goal, Rinse, Repeat

Goal setting is not a once-a-year endeavor. It is an ongoing practice to ensure your team is focused on the critical priorities. When teams are busy and productivity is high, you assume the work is getting done, so why worry about goals?

Without well-defined goals, teams are forced to react to the latest big idea, execution suffers as employees grapple with vying priorities, and organizations often report lost productivity and low employee morale. Your team needs clear expectations along with clear-cut direction. This was not the case with Sara and Ethan. Ethan had committed to a series of actions. However, there was no agreement as to the end result and what would constitute success. Goal setting is critical in any coaching you do.

The key to achieving those results is to ensure there is clarity.

I Can See Clearly Now

It is critical to help the employee set goals, identify the outcome and its associated steps, and determine how success will be measured in the targeted area. Without this, focus diminishes, motivation wanes, and the path to their goal becomes unclear.

After all, you, as the leader coach, have the big-picture view. You know the anticipated result and how it will impact all involved. So, how do you help your employee develop goals to achieve a desired outcome? The answers to these six questions will help bring the clarity you need.

1. What do you want to do?
2. What is your desired outcome(s)?
3. What specific steps will you take?
4. What obstacles stand in your way?
5. What is the time frame associated with this goal?
6. How will you measure success?

Take a look at each of these areas to see how they drive clarity when setting goals.

1. **What do you want to do?** Counsel your employee to think through the goals that will help them achieve success. The employee should commit to a goal they have a reasonable level of confidence in achieving. Having a stretch goal—an ambitious or challenging goal—promotes learning, but it should be practical, otherwise it can discourage action. Have them respond to the statement *"I will do the following . . ."*

2. **What is your desired outcome(s)?** It's important for the employee to have clarity around what they will gain upon achieving the goal. Help them

understand the reason they are undertaking this goal in the first place. The employee should be able to validate, *"This is important because I will gain these benefits . . ."*

3. **What specific steps will you take?** Encourage them to outline the specific steps they will take to reach the desired result. They need to separate things into manageable steps and consider short-term and long-term actions. More about this in a moment. They should be able to articulate, *"The specific steps I will take include . . ."*

4. **What obstacles stand in your way?** It is difficult to plan for the unknown. However, proactively thinking through the actions to take if something stands in the way helps the employee plan for the unexpected. The employee will be compelled to think through what they will do or whom they can enlist to help them when they confront an obstacle. This helps the employee determine, *"What I will do when I encounter a roadblock . . ."* or *"Whom I will reach out to when I encounter a roadblock . . ."*

5. **What is the time frame associated with this goal?** Inspire the employee to set a time frame that establishes a sense of urgency and ensures they are working toward a deadline. The hardest part of achieving goals is typically getting started. This helps the employee think through, *"I will start this on . . ."* and *"I will finish this on . . ."*

6. **How will you measure success?** Your employee should determine the criteria for how success will be measured toward achieving the desired goal. Here is where you build accountability by asking questions to help the employee establish measures and milestones

that will lead to success. This is the time to ask your employee if they are fully committed to take the necessary steps to achieve their goal. *"The following criteria or milestones will constitute my success . . ."* The employee should also be able to identify, *"The following people can provide feedback on my progress . . ."*

You can use the following chart to facilitate these discussions and assist your employees with setting goals. Refer to the six questions to complete this.

Goal	Desired Outcome	Key Steps	Overcoming Obstacles	Time Frame	Measures of Success
1.					
2.					
3.					
4.					
5.					

By investing time to answer these questions and set goals at this stage, the employee will be more likely to stick with their plan and will be more successful in achieving what they set out to achieve. In the next chapter, we will look at Execution and additional data points to help you and the employee answer these questions.

The Cure for Indecisiveness

Setting short-term and long-term goals helps the employee determine the level of effort required to expedite a goal and the resources needed to accomplish this, versus what needs a more measured approach. Short-term goals are typically achieved in six months or less, whereas long-term goals often take over six months to achieve.

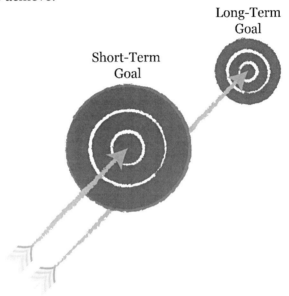

Separating goals into short-term and long-term also helps the employee evaluate the level of urgency. If a fast turnaround is required, but it is not the best solution, the request can be met in the short term while the employee works on a more advantageous solution for the long term.

Furthermore, setting short-term goals can motivate an employee to reach a long-term goal that might feel out of reach, such as developing the necessary skills to delegate. Sometimes an employee is indecisive and unsure how to proceed in accomplishing a goal.

This can happen for any number of reasons, including:

~ The goal is too enormous to accomplish all at once.
~ An ideal solution is unavailable.
~ A quick fix is needed to fulfill a need within an organization.

In this regard, suggest the employee establish a short-term goal, one measured in days or weeks, that helps them divide things into more manageable steps. Establishing a short-term goal enables the employee to make progress, in phases, while identifying a path to achieve the longer-term strategy. On the other hand, an ideal solution may not be readily available, or a quick fix is needed, rendering the short-term goal an interim step until the longer-term goal can be achieved.

However, not every goal needs to be accomplished immediately. Similarly, not every goal should take months or years to accomplish. Once you and your employee establish goals, determine which actions have the highest priority and which ones can be accomplished later.

Rewind: Success for the Long Term

Having explored a variety of alternatives, Ethan tells Sara which option he believes is most ideal to pursue. As Sara nods in agreement, he feels confident that he can work with his team to make it happen. Surprisingly, Ethan hasn't felt this confident about delegating in a long time.

After Ethan explains his course of action, Sara replies, "You've given this a lot of thought in the short term. What would it look like longer term? How will you sustain delegating?"

Ethan hadn't considered his strategy beyond his

immediate tasks, yet he realizes he needs to identify his longer-term goals. He knows he has a tendency to delegate initially, but when a new request surfaces, his resolve weakens and he fails to follow through. As a result, he feels overwhelmed and ends up working long hours. He has done that too many times before, so he admits that not having both a short- and long-term plan could set him and his team up for failure.

As he thinks about the multiple steps required to accomplish his goals, Ethan considers the prospect of delegating work on a regular basis. With so many moving parts, and so many people involved, he wonders how he will know the status if he assigns those tasks to his team.

As if reading his mind, Sara asks, "What would need to be in place for you to let more responsibilities go and sustain this over time?"

They brainstorm additional options and arrive at several viable solutions. Ethan now feels he has a good handle on the specific steps to take, how he will delegate tasks, which elements he will measure, and what his timeline is.

Before Ethan leaves, Sara brings the conversation back to his career aspirations. She asks him a final question: "How will the actions you plan to take help you meet your long-term goal to take on greater responsibility?"

Ethan shares how his ability to delegate and sustain this plan will help him meet his goal. He feels energized with a solid plan and Sara's support to be successful in his endeavors. He is ready to get started.

Connect the Dots

This opportunity enabled Sara and Ethan to envision the future by achieving short-term as well as long-term career goals.

Tie this step to the employee's career goal. The career goal is typically the longer-term goal, such as the desire to take on a larger team and greater responsibility. The short-term goals are the areas to develop to meet this longer-term goal, such as delegating work in the short term and sustaining this over time. As the leader coach, you need to ensure the employee never loses sight of how their development (short-term) relates to their (long-term) career goal.

Here are some questions you can ask at the Goal-Setting stage.

- Which option makes the most sense right now?
- What do you want to do, short-term and long-term?
- What three goals do you want to set for yourself?
- I notice there are times you struggle with making the final decision. What support do you need from me?
- What steps do you want to take?
- What obstacles stand in your way?
- What is the outcome you want to achieve?
- How will these actions help you meet your goals?

In the next chapter, we will build on the goal-setting stage by establishing measures and milestones to assist in achieving these goals.

Please visit www.thesagealliance.com/worksheets for a list of questions that will assist you at this stage in the coaching process.

Your Call to Action

Reflections I Will Take

Which step(s) will help you facilitate goal setting? Check as many as apply.

- ☐ Collaborate to establish clear goals with a positive outcome
- ☐ Set short-term goals to foster immediate action
- ☐ Help with identifying long-term goals
- ☐ Assist with connecting short-term goals to (long-term) career goals

Actions I Will Take

1. Schedule a one-on-one with each of your employees and have an in-depth discussion of their strengths, development opportunities, and where they see themselves next in their career. Many leaders do this annually at review time; however, it's imperative to have this conversation outside of salary review and focus on the employee and their aspirations for the coming months. What strengths and cautions of your leader coach style (Analytical, Results, People, Thought) will impact your success?

2. If you have recently had this discussion, then ensure you zero in on the employee's desired career goal. This can be a promotion, taking on more responsibility, learning a new skill, closing a gap, or something else.

   This should be a future goal that you and the employee can work on together over the next year. As you coach the employee day to day, make a concerted effort to tie the short-term goal to their larger career goal.

3. Share the six questions found in this chapter with your employees to facilitate setting goals. Use the My Execution Plan template, which can be found at www.thesagealliance.com/worksheets. This will help them gain clarity and enable you to coach them more effectively. Refer to the six questions earlier in this chapter for assistance in completing this exercise.

Go to www.thesagealliance.com/worksheets to download the following coaching worksheet that will help you conduct your one-on-one conversations.

sage
alliance

One-on-One Coaching Tracking Form

Employee Name:

Career Goals
1.
2.
3.

Strengths

Development Opportunities

Areas for Coaching (Behaviors Impacting Achievement of Goals)

Meeting Notes

© Sage Alliance 2019

www.thesagealliance.com

Execution and Accountability: How Things Get Done

A goal made but not acted upon is as useless as a goal never set.

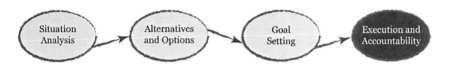

As decisions get more and more complex, employees hesitate when it comes to taking action. They fear taking a risk, making a mistake, or even worse, being admonished for proceeding without consulting you first. The SAGE Coaching Approach streamlines this process and mitigates the risk, clearing the way for confident decision making and execution to ensure employees reach their goals.

A goal made but not acted upon is as useless as a goal never set. Execution is the key to success. It is how you and your team reach your desired results. It is how you grow as a leader coach, and how you help your employees grow as leaders.

You Think You're Coaching: Sara and Ethan

Ethan knows the next steps he should take to begin delegating. Sara is anxious for Ethan to make progress. She wants to ensure he's successful by helping him stay on track.

"Ethan, I will check in at the end of the week to see how you are progressing. Also, get on my calendar for thirty minutes every Friday, so you can update me on your progress over the week and discuss any challenges you've encountered."

Ethan agrees to Sara's request and appreciates her support.

What is a better way for Sara to coach Ethan on executing successfully and remaining accountable?

Don't Get Cold Feet

In this phase of the SAGE Coaching Approach, you will assist the employee with identifying their action plan and the obstacles that stand in their way. Helping the employee think through these steps will reduce frustration, yours and theirs, and will steer them on a productive path. In this example with Ethan, Sara is still driving the outcome. She is dictating the follow-up meetings as a means to ensure things stay on track instead of coaching around actions and fostering ownership if Ethan hits a roadblock. Ethan will continue to rely on Sara to solve his problems without any real commitment to how he is going to reach his goals.

A key component to effective execution is accountability and ensuring the employee is willing to accept responsibility for the key actions they need to take. Their willingness to make the commitment and follow through on those commitments is strengthened through your coaching. You've had great conversations up to this point, but without accountability, ownership can suffer, jeopardizing successful execution. Let's see how Sara handles this with Ethan.

Rewind: Get 'er Done

By now, Ethan is feeling great about what he and Sara have discussed. He knows the next steps he should take, including which team members will do which tasks, how and when they will communicate their progress to him, and the best way to track that progress. In his four years at the company, he has never felt this empowered and ready to begin delegating.

"Okay, I think I've got it," he says. "I'm ready to go!" Ethan gathers his notes and heads for the door.

"Before you go, Ethan, when would you like to circle back to touch base on your progress?" Sara asks.

This idea of touching base with Sara along the way makes sense to Ethan. Rather than coming to her for advice each and every time he encounters a roadblock, he realizes regular check-ins will be an opportunity to discuss his progress and demonstrate his ability to make the necessary changes to prepare him for the next step in his career.

Once they decide on a meeting schedule, Sara leaves him with a few final questions to ponder. "Ethan, what stands in the way of you succeeding long term? Think of it like this: on a scale of one to ten, what's the likelihood of you following through in the manner we've discussed?"

These are tough questions, but Ethan is glad Sara has asked them. He knows he needs this kind of deep thinking to move him forward in his career. He thinks long and hard. "Well, nothing really stands in my way. I'm sure I can make this plan happen," he says. "If I had to guess on its likelihood, considering everything, I'd say we're at a seven." He wishes the number were higher, but he knows it will take some time to bring his team up to speed on all the various initiatives and for him to feel comfortable with them taking the lead.

Sara knows this is hard for Ethan but asks him, "What would make it a ten?"

He knows this new approach is a big step. In the past, he has been so used to reacting to short-term issues that he hasn't had the chance to think long term. He explains that he needs to get started and see how the plan unfolds over the next few weeks, then make some adjustments. Maybe then he will feel more confident rating the effort a ten.

Sara asks one final question. "Okay, what support do you need from me?"

Ethan has gotten so much out of this meeting that he suggests a similar structure for their weekly meetings. "I really appreciate all the questions you've asked me today. They really took me outside my comfort zone and made me think of solutions I didn't realize were in front of me the whole time."

Sara agrees. "I know you can do it, Ethan!"

Convert Discussions to Action

Creating a plan for execution and accountability might seem

intuitive, but this is often overlooked. Now is the time to convert a productive discussion into action that clearly aligns with the goals established in the prior step.

As a manager, you might be used to leading the discussion at this point and telling the employee when you should meet again. You have good intentions; however, this approach puts you in control, thwarts ownership, and curtails the employee's growth.

Continue to ask thought-provoking questions to promote action. Prompt the employee to suggest timing for status and update meetings by asking, "When do you want to meet again?" Entrust the employee with the authority and ultimate ownership for these meetings. This will ensure they will be prepared to highlight their progress and identify concerns they want to address.

Formalize measurements and timing by encouraging employees to take the necessary action. Provide the guidance and hold them accountable for following through. Explore the support they need to be successful, while offering encouragement along the way.

Actions Speak Louder Than Words

There are several steps you can take to ensure effective execution at this stage in your coaching. The following provides guidelines to avoid the common pitfalls that can derail success.

~ Clarify Ownership and Accountability
~ Specify Measurements and Milestones
~ Make the Goal Actionable
~ Be Fully Committed
~ Establish Clear Expectations
~ Offer Encouragement and Motivation

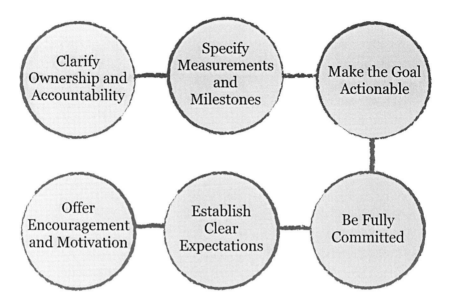

Let's look at each of the steps to ensure effective execution.

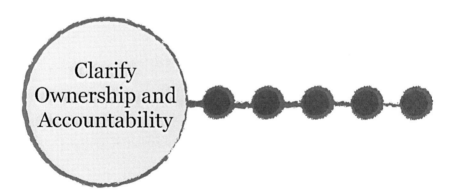

Being clear about next steps is essential to ensuring the employee is, in fact, taking ownership of the process and has accepted their role to be accountable for the wins, misses, and outcomes of an initiative.

When an employee is uncertain of how to implement a long-range goal, the moment they hit a bump in the road, they will consult you for advice. They need to come up with their *own* plan for overcoming this obstacle. If you define the plan, at the first instance of a roadblock, they may veer off from your intended trajectory. You see, this is *your* plan, not the employee's.

For true accountability and ownership, the employee must come up with the solution. There are times where this is not feasible, such as if the employee really does not know the steps to take. A coaching approach provides the employee the encouragement they need and a sounding board to brainstorm options to help them get back on course.

By understanding the specific steps the employee will take, they will accept responsibility for ownership and follow-up. As with the other steps in the SAGE Coaching Approach, asking open-ended questions and being curious is the most effective route to ensure the employee has thought through the ramifications and stays on track.

Questions include:

- What specifically are you going to do? When will you do it?
- What else do you need to be successful here?
- What support do you need from me?
- How do you want to be held accountable?
- On a scale of 1–10, what's the likelihood of you doing this?
- If deadlines or milestones are missed, how do you want me to hold you accountable?
- How will you ensure ownership on your team?
- How will you hold your team accountable?

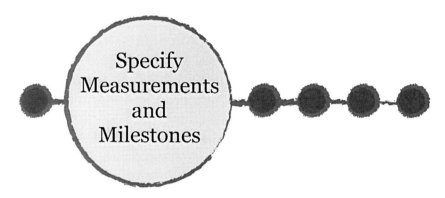

Specify
Measurements
and
Milestones

All too often when you discuss development opportunities, the employee will enthusiastically agree to take action; however, the measures for success have not been established. Without these measures and the associated milestones, this diminishes accountability and can set the employee up for failure. We saw this with Ethan when he agreed to delegate *more*.

How is *more* measured? If Ethan delegates one project, is that more? Of course it is, but is that the outcome Sara is hoping he will achieve?

Establish measurements at this stage to ensure you and the employee are in agreement with which elements will be evaluated and how they, and you, will know when success has been achieved. With most initiatives, that requires multiple steps, stages, and long-term planning; establishing the milestones the employee will reach along the way brings clarity at the start of the initiative. This also provides employees with guidelines for measurement throughout the process, and motivation to continue their successful execution.

Questions to ask to establish measurements include:

- ~ You stated you want to do more of xyz. What constitutes *more*?
- ~ What signifies success for you?
- ~ How will we measure success?

- ～ What criteria or guidelines will you use to achieve your goal?
- ～ What do you want to achieve short term? Long term?
- ～ What milestones do you want to establish to reach your goal?
- ～ Describe what success looks like if you achieve this.

Make the Goal Actionable

Previously we discussed the importance of ownership and accountability. Now is the time to discuss how to make their goals actionable. Oftentimes, managers get this far in their coaching, yet do not encourage the employee to make the plan actionable. You agree on the outcome, but the employee leaves feeling uncertain of the next steps or how to get started.

Merely having a conversation about the end result does not guarantee the actions the employee is committing to are clear. They may still be unsure *how* to accomplish the task, or may have trepidation on taking a particular course of action.

This confusion occurs when you brainstorm ideas, but they are not specific enough to make them actionable. As the leader coach, you want the employee to communicate the specific steps they will take. This helps them gain clarity, and demonstrates their commitment to the process and how they will achieve their goals. It also helps you know what to watch out for and determine consequences associated with missed deadlines and milestones, as well as encouragement for accomplishments.

Questions you can incorporate to ensure the conversation is actionable:

~ What specific actions do you want to take?
~ What steps will you take?
~ What is your action plan?
~ What are you committing to do?
~ When will you get started?
~ When will you complete this?
~ What will you do and when will you do it?

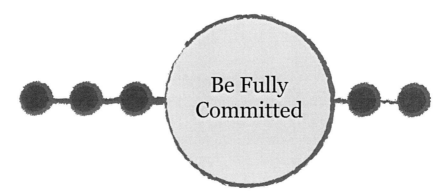

Be Fully
Committed

There are times when employees genuinely believe they can or will do an activity, but they do not follow through. How many times have you committed to lose weight or exercise or restrain from eating unhealthy food? What got in your way? Everyone makes commitments, with good intentions. Unfortunately, we do not always think through the ramifications associated with taking a particular course of action.

The focus of your coaching at this juncture should not be on whether the employee knows what steps to take, but rather whether they are committed to taking those steps. Are they willing to do whatever it takes to reach the goal, regardless of the ramifications? There are bound to be obstacles along the way.

Discuss these obstacles up front with your employee to ensure expectations are realistic. Ask questions to determine how they will respond to obstacles, whether they will give up upon reaching a roadblock or soldier on, if they will make the tough decision and take on the inherent risk, and whether they have thought through what it will take to be successful.

If the employee is not fully committed to do what they agreed to, it is probably not going to get accomplished. In many instances, the issue could be a specific obstacle the employee is uncertain of how to overcome, and this will stop them from making progress. Once you identify this obstacle and determine the key actions, the next step is to set milestones and measures. One of my favorite coaching questions is actually a series of three questions:

1. What will you do?
2. When will you do it?
3. How will you let me know?

This establishes the specific action the employee will take. The time frame is identified for when they will take that action. And lastly, the method for when they will update you on their progress is clear.

Here are some questions you can ask to ascertain the employee's commitment level:

~ What obstacles stand in your way?
~ What support do you need from me to be successful?
~ What will you do if things don't work out as planned?
~ On a scale of 1–10, what is the likelihood of you doing this?
~ What prevents it from being a 10?

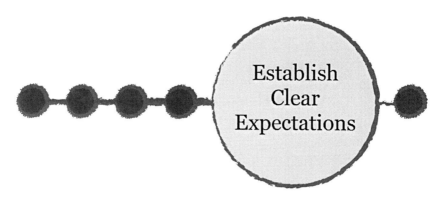

Establish
Clear
Expectations

Follow-ups and check-ins are critical for you to determine the status of the project and receive updates on progress. But *you* should not initiate these check-ins. The employee should proactively update you. You should not have to follow up with them. Encourage the employee to be accountable and take ownership for scheduling meetings with you, outside of regularly scheduled times.

This may seem like a minor point; however, this is a good indicator to determine if expectations are clear. State up front that you would like them to update you on their progress. If the time frame they choose does not meet your expectations, explain you need higher frequency.

If you're constantly checking in, then clear expectations have not been set as to how the employee should update and communicate their progress. You are sabotaging their accountability and enabling their dependence on you to solve the problem. When this happens, you are managing, rather than being a leader coach.

Important as it is for the employee to initiate check-ins, you need to feel comfortable letting go, certain that your initial discussion has laid a solid groundwork for the employee to accomplish the agreed-upon tasks and report their progress to you.

Some questions to set clear expectations include:

- ~ When will we meet again?
- ~ How do you want to update me on your progress?
- ~ When will you update me on your progress?
- ~ How will you communicate delays or obstacles?
- ~ I haven't received an update from you. What needs to be in place to ensure I receive these updates in the future?

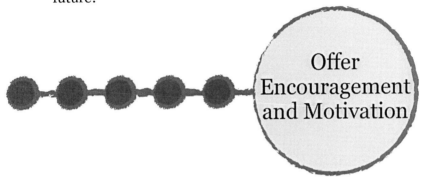

Offer
Encouragement
and Motivation

Lastly, do not overlook the importance of encouragement and motivation. In all likelihood, the initiative or task the employee is embarking on is a growth opportunity that will take them out of their comfort zone. Therefore, they still need some indication that you support them and believe in their ability to accomplish the initiatives as agreed. This is where encouragement and motivation come in.

Although encouragement and motivation may seem insignificant to you, they can be critical to your employees. Recognizing that what the employee is undertaking may be difficult for them accomplishes two goals: 1) it provides encouragement for them to proceed, and 2) it motivates them to see the task or initiative through to the end, despite the obstacles.

For these tactics to be most effective, you must be authentic. This does not mean making statements that you are uncomfortable with. Be honest, truthful, and genuine in your communications to ensure employees recognize that you care about them as a person, not just as an employee.

By expressing your confidence in them, you motivate your team and encourage them to achieve their goals.

Examples of encouraging phrases include but are not limited to:

- I know you can do it!
- You are capable of more than you think.
- I believe in you.
- I trust your judgment.
- I've got your back.
- You have the skill and ability to do this.
- I have confidence in your abilities.
- Look how much you have already accomplished.
- You are on the path to reach your goal of . . .
- Accomplishing this will help you operate more effectively at the next level of leadership.

Implementing the SAGE Coaching Approach will:

- Improve problem-solving and decision-making skills with your employees
- Encourage your team to act decisively, despite complexity and uncertainty
- Instill ownership and accountability
- Ensure execution is successful

Visit www.thesagealliance.com/worksheets for a list of questions that will assist you at this stage in the coaching process.

Your Call to Action

Reflections I Will Make

What will you do to improve your coaching around Execution

and Accountability? Think about the areas where you want to assist your team to execute successfully, take ownership, and remain accountable. Check all the boxes that apply.

- ☐ Clarify ownership and accountability
- ☐ Specify measurements and milestones
- ☐ Facilitate an agreed-upon timeline to make it actionable
- ☐ Determine how committed the employee is to taking action
- ☐ Establish clear expectations for communications
- ☐ Offer encouragement and motivation

Actions I Will Take

1. Write down the area(s) in this list that is most challenging for you. Set a goal for what you will specifically do to improve in each of the areas you chose. What strengths and cautions of your leader coach style (Analytical, Results, People, Thought) will impact your success?

2. Develop a list of questions that will help you ensure execution and accountability will be successful. Make these questions your own. The objective is to find out up front where a person is struggling, or where they may seem committed but are not.

3. Think about the current state. How often do you provide encouragement? What are some strategies you will use to turn up the volume and offer additional encouragement?

Go to www.thesagealliance.com/worksheets to download the following worksheet that will help you chart your progress.

SAGE Coaching Approach

Use this worksheet to plan out your next coaching conversation. Write the questions you will ask in the spaces provided.

Situation Analysis
- What's the current situation?
- What is your assessment of what's going on?
- Where do you need help?
- What are you struggling with the most right now?
- What is getting in the way of success?
- What obstacles are standing in your way?
- What is stopping you from making this decision?
- What have you already tried? What is the impact?
- What do you make of all this?
- How do you want it to be if all goes as planned?

Alternatives and Options
- What have you thought about or already tried?
- What do you think could work here?
- What other options can you think of?
- What could you do differently?
- That's one option, what's another?
- What are the pros and cons (of each option)?
- What would happen if you do nothing?
- What needs to be in place for you to be successful?
- How do you want to rank these options?

Goal Setting
- Which option makes the most sense right now?
- What do you want to do, short term and long term?
- What three goals do you want to set for yourself?
- I notice there are times you struggle with making the final decision. What support do you need from me?
- What steps do you want to take?
- How will these actions help you meet your goals?
- What obstacles stand in your way?
- What is the outcome you want to achieve?

Execution and Accountability
- On a scale of 1–10, what's the likelihood of you doing this? What prevents it from being a 10?
- When will you get started?
- What support do you need from me?
- How will we measure success?
- When will we follow up/meet again?
- What will you do and when will you do it?
- I noticed you didn't do what you said you would do, how do you want to be held accountable?
- What will you do if things don't work out as planned?
- I know you can do it! I believe in you!

www.thesagealliance.com

Transform
to Leader Coach

The Feedback Loop

Before you can move the employee to action, you will sometimes need to deliver targeted feedback and then coach them based on the outcomes you collectively agree for them to reach.

Giving tough feedback can be stressful for most people. Many managers are truly conflict-averse and avoid giving feedback like the plague. You want to achieve results, yet you do not want to hurt someone's feelings, or worse, cause someone to be defensive. You may have even established friendships with employees on your team and you don't want to jeopardize those relationships.

Giving feedback can conjure up feelings of fear and trepidation, so it takes courage. Many leaders are apprehensive of their employees' reactions, in the form of defensiveness, emotional outbursts, or negativity. You don't want to hurt someone's feelings intentionally or feel awkward while giving feedback. But how else can you develop your team if you do not provide honest feedback?

The simple truth is employees want to know how they are performing, even if the way they receive it is perceived as negative. The only way they will grow is by getting feedback. Without it, employees are less engaged, and they do not perceive they are learning and developing their leadership capabilities.

The Feedback Dichotomy

There are times when you will need to give corrective feedback to coach an employee more effectively. You might observe behaviors that are getting in the way of the employee's success. If you don't bring these behaviors to the surface, you will not be effective in coaching them to improve. In this case, before you can move the employee to action, you will sometimes need to deliver targeted feedback and then coach them based on the outcomes you collectively agree for them to reach.

You may naturally assume your employee does not want to receive redirecting (corrective) feedback, but that is far from the case. Most employees know this feedback is critical for them to improve and take on additional challenges. However, although they desire the corrective feedback, they may not like it. For most people, receiving feedback is uncomfortable and awkward. But most employees know it is essential to develop further in their career. Why is there such a dichotomy between liking feedback and wanting feedback?

When employees are asked what was most helpful in their career, 72 percent thought their performance would improve if their managers provided corrective feedback. But how it was done mattered, according to 92 percent of employees who agreed with the assertion. Negative (redirecting) feedback, *if delivered appropriately*, is effective at improving performance.[1]

In many organizations, feedback is reserved for the annual review, since this is positioned to benchmark the employee's performance. This can make you hesitate to give corrective feedback and guidance in the moment that would otherwise help your employees to continue to develop throughout the year.

For the employee, receiving feedback gets a bad name because so many leaders avoid regularly giving redirecting, corrective feedback, or any feedback for that matter. When employees receive redirecting feedback at the annual review, they are oftentimes surprised about what they did incorrectly and baffled why they had not received any indication prior.

Employee engagement goes up dramatically when employees receive regular feedback, even when it is centered around their weaknesses. Employees who receive daily feedback from their managers are three times more likely to be engaged than those who receive feedback once a year or less.[2] Feedback highlights behavior to continue (reinforcing) or to modify (redirecting) to be more effective. Without constructive feedback, you are impeding the opportunity for employees to self-correct, improve their performance, and experience a sense of accomplishment and growth.

How feedback is given matters. Keep these best practices in mind:

1. Provide feedback immediately or within a twenty-four-hour period for the greatest impact. The immediacy will be dictated by whether it is an appropriate time, whether you and the employee are available to speak, and whether you are in the frame of mind to provide such feedback. Preparation will help with this latter point. The longer you wait, the less effective your feedback will be.

2. Always provide feedback in private, one on one. This applies to both reinforcing and redirecting feedback. You do not want to pinpoint areas for development in a meeting or in front of the employee's colleagues. By the same token, many people are uncomfortable receiving positive feedback, especially in a group setting. It will seem more genuine and allow the employee to accept the feedback more readily when it is done in private.

3. Ask the employee how they like to receive feedback. This enables you to understand their comfort level, whether they need you to soften the delivery, or if they need additional time to process what they heard. This helps establish trust, openness, and receptiveness to feedback.

We will look at a proven approach that will help you gain greater conviction with providing feedback later in this chapter.

Many executives I coach share this sentiment: "I gave feedback to one of my employees, but they have not made any of the needed changes to address the issue we discussed." The leader is frustrated. The employee confirmed they understood the feedback. So, why has the employee not made the necessary changes in their behavior? Feedback alone is not enough to change behaviors.

An employee may recognize they need to make a change, but if they knew how to do it, they would probably already be doing it. They need help to implement the change, which is often the step you left out of their feedback discussion. Don't confuse feedback for coaching; they are different. So, what does it mean to give feedback, and how is feedback tied to coaching?

You Think You're Coaching: Sara and Ethan

What a week—meeting after meeting after meeting. This new initiative requires all hands on deck and hours of back-to-back meetings. As Sara reflects on the meetings over the past week, she recognizes numerous opportunities where Ethan answered questions on his team's behalf or interrupted them to provide the right answer. She knows she needs to give Ethan this feedback; however, she doesn't want this to overshadow all the great progress he has made in delegating.

Sara knows he has good intentions but that he probably doesn't realize what he is doing and how this is counterproductive for his team's development. She provides this feedback in their biweekly one-on-one.

"Ethan, you have been doing such a great job delegating. I've seen your team taking on additional initiatives, and I see things progressing forward. Congratulations!

"*But* I've noticed you tend to take control in meetings and not let your team answer questions on their own. For them to feel fully in charge, they need to learn how to manage situations where they may not always know the answer to questions.

"Continue all the great delegating you are doing. Just make sure you are letting them take the lead when questions are posed in meetings."

Ethan ponders Sara's feedback. He agrees he needs to develop his team more, but he's confused on what he is doing well and the areas he needs to improve. He's unsure how to implement Sara's recommendations.

Let's look at a better way for Sara to communicate her expectations with Ethan, ensure he understands the areas for improvement, and for her to feel more comfortable and prepared while giving targeted feedback.

OWN It!

When you give feedback, your employees feel inspired to make the necessary shifts and appreciate the investment you make in them. My proprietary OWN Formula helps pave the way for you to provide targeted feedback and feel more at ease while doing so.

OWN it!

Observations → Why → Next Steps

O: Observations
W: Why
N: Next Steps

This formula works for positive, reinforcing feedback as well as corrective, redirecting feedback. You simply need to *OWN* it and do it!

Observations

Describe the behavior you observe. Cite specific examples of the behavior you want them to either continue doing, or to address and correct. All too often, employees receive vague feedback that leaves them questioning what or where they need to improve.

As an example: "You don't speak up enough in meetings." The employee does not have the necessary insight into what they need to change or how to change it. Is it during specific meetings you want them to speak up more? What does speaking up more look like for the employee? By giving specific examples, the employee can gain greater understanding of what behavior you are asking them to modify. Instead, coach them by asking targeted questions. Consider this: "What would you need to feel comfortable sharing your point of view in our team meetings?"

Avoid unconstructive statements such as, "You are so timid. Just yesterday you didn't speak up in our team meeting." This can cause the employee to become defensive and not internalize your feedback. Focus on what you observed and avoid making it personal by associating labels to the behavior.

An example of what *to do* is:

"In yesterday's team meeting, there was an opportunity for you to share your opinion on the strategy with the rest of the team. When I asked if anyone had any input on our strategy, you remained quiet and didn't share your point of view."

This provides an opportunity for the employee to address why they did not speak up and share their concerns with the manager. It is important to focus on the specific and observable behavior and not to make it personal.

Why Is This Important?

Once you have shared examples of the behavior you want to address, describe why it is important for you to give this feedback in the first place. Also, describe the impact this behavior has on you as the manager, on the team, morale, etc.

An example of this is:

"When you don't speak up, your colleagues assume you don't have an opinion or the knowledge on a topic. As a result, decisions are made without your team members seeking your input. The impact of not speaking up is that members on the team don't view you as knowledgeable about the market, and they may discount your opinion in the future. This is important for you to address since you're interested in taking on additional responsibilities. Having your voice heard on our ongoing strategy will be critical to your success for you to gain buy-in, earn stakeholder support, and be seen as a trusted resource."

Next Steps

Once the impact is understood, now is the time to discuss the specific actions the employee can take, or behaviors they need to modify to address this feedback. All too often, managers give feedback, but they do not discuss alternatives and options with the employee. During this phase, the employee is aware of the behavior, but needs some guidance in how to make the necessary behavior changes.

Depending on the feedback and the behavior you are addressing with the employee, Next Steps might be more directive in how they need to develop further. As an example, if someone is continually late for meetings, you will need them to agree they will not be late in the future. You might even suggest they allow more time between meetings to ensure they arrive on time.

However, in most cases you will begin coaching. In our example with the employee who does not speak up in meetings, you want to gain a better understanding of what is holding them back from sharing their opinion. Ask clarifying questions to determine if the deterrent is insufficient knowledge, lack of confidence, fear of looking stupid (in front of their peers), compulsion to make fact-based recommendations (or feeling they will suffer negative consequences), or something else.

If you assume you know why a behavior is happening, such as why the employee is not speaking up, you are not coaching them on the root cause.

Examples of questions you can ask at this juncture include:

- What is holding you back from speaking up?
- Would you like to brainstorm on some options that will help you feel more comfortable speaking up?
- What is the worst thing that can happen if you say something others disagree with?

Feedback and coaching work together, in essence like two gears. There are times when you will need to gain a deeper understanding of the Situation. Here, you want to understand the root cause of a specific behavior, as in our example of the employee who does not speak up in meetings. Other times, once you provide feedback, you will pick up with brainstorming Alternatives and Options before setting Goals. Regardless of where you begin, you will move to the next phase in the SAGE Coaching Approach and work through to Execution and Accountability.

Don't confuse giving feedback with coaching. Feedback is critical, but without coaching to brainstorm options, set goals, and reinforce the behavior, the employee will be indecisive and puzzled with how to implement the new behavior.

Rewind: Toughen Up

Sara prepared for her meeting with Ethan and is ready to provide him with OWN feedback.

"Ethan, what I **Observed** in yesterday's meeting is you

took control of the conversation when members of your team hesitated after I asked them a question. You cut them off and didn't give them an opportunity to respond when you interjected with the answer.

"**Why** is this important for us to discuss today?

"When you cut members of your team off and supply the answer, this causes them to become reticent to speak up. This stifles their ability to take initiative when you're in the room and directly impacts your ability to delegate more authority to them.

"The longer-term impact is they will not feel confident to answer questions, as they will expect you to respond on their behalf. They will not truly have ownership of the projects, nor will they feel empowered. This will jeopardize their success when you delegate to them. They'll continue to rely on you, and you'll lose confidence in their ability to take ownership and see the project through to completion.

"Let's discuss some **Next Steps.** Would you like to brainstorm some options for when you feel yourself getting impatient and wanting to provide the answer on behalf of your team?"

It's a Balancing Act

Feedback is critical for your team to gain greater self-awareness, address troublesome behaviors, and continue to learn and grow. Remember, feedback is a balance. Don't miss out on opportunities to recognize good behavior, superior performance, and stellar accomplishments. Without this, your team will see you as overlooking all the positive effort they make and focus only on when something goes astray.

The OWN Formula is exceedingly effective for positive, reinforcing behavior as well. When you provide positive feedback, as stated earlier, the team is engaged, motivated, productive, and innovative.

Here's an example of a conversation that uses positive, reinforcing feedback:

"You shared a lot of significant ideas in today's meeting that helped the team make progress on this initiative." (**O**bservations)

"The team appreciated your input and sees you as a valuable resource. This positioned you as the subject matter expert in this area and will ensure you're kept in the loop when similar initiatives arise." (**W**hy)

"Continue looking for opportunities where you can leverage your knowledge and expertise." (**N**ext Steps)

Be proactive identifying opportunities to give positive feedback. This will provide the needed balance and will create a feedback culture where employees will be more open to receiving corrective, redirecting feedback when you do a good job of giving positive feedback to reward good behavior.

Here are three helpful tips for using OWN:

1. Keep the focus on the specific behavior you observed, not on the person, how you feel about them, or how they are approaching the task. If the feedback is mixed in with additional sentiments, the redirecting (corrective) feedback will get lost. This is confusing for the employee and does not empower them to take the necessary steps to correct the behavior.

2. Highlight the impact to you as the manager, the team, the organization, morale, and anyone else who is affected by the behavior you observed. Be as specific as possible. Help the employee understand how their behavior positively or negatively influences building relationships, fostering trust, gaining buy-in, and guaranteeing the overall success of an initiative.

3. Make your feedback actionable. There are times when feedback is more directive, and other times when you will brainstorm options. In either instance, avoid vague statements that offer no clear expectation of needed improvement and desired results. Regardless of how you get to the solution, agree on how you will measure success and when you expect to discuss progress.

Feedback alone is not enough to change an employee's behavior. Time and time again, managers question why an employee has not modified their behavior when they have provided corrective feedback. This is because feedback must be combined with coaching. Coaching will address the *why,* i.e. the impact as explained in the OWN Formula. For feedback to work, it also needs to address *how* to approach changing the behavior. This is where the SAGE Coaching Approach comes in.

Want to build a high-performing team that overcomes obstacles, surpasses expectations, achieves their goals, and delivers superior results? Enable them through building a culture of feedback. What I mean by this is a culture that promotes giving feedback as a regular occurrence and not solely reserved for annual reviews. To develop your employees and build a high-performing team, it's important to give them regular and timely feedback.

Feedback is a two-way street. Don't overlook the importance of asking for feedback from your employees, especially as you make the shift to leader coach. This is an excellent opportunity to receive specific and targeted feedback on capabilities you can develop and approaches that result in your improvement as a leader coach. When you demonstrate your willingness to receive feedback, you create a positive culture where this is appreciated. In turn, this primes your team to be open to feedback as well.

Your Call to Action

Reflections I Will Make

In which areas do you want to improve providing feedback? Check all that apply.

- ☐ Provide more positive, reinforcing feedback
- ☐ Identify opportunities to redirect behavior through corrective feedback
- ☐ Use OWN to get more comfortable and prepare for giving feedback
- ☐ Encourage team to provide you feedback using OWN
- ☐ Provide feedback to address behaviors and coach next steps so the employee knows how to proceed

Actions I Will Take

1. Identify opportunities to provide your team with feedback. OWN can be used for both reinforcing (positive) and redirecting (corrective) feedback. Choose a situation where you will give a team member reinforcing feedback using OWN. This is an opportunity to reinforce a positive behavior you have observed, and you want them to continue in this vein. Consider the following in your feedback:

O: What I observed is . . .
W: Why this is important is because . . .
N: Some next steps include . . .

Reflect on the outcome. What else will you do to be effective giving reinforcing feedback? What are additional opportunities for you to reinforce positive behavior?

2. Identify an opportunity to provide redirecting feedback to someone on your team. Once you have observed a behavior you would like them to address and modify, consider the following in your feedback:

O: What I observed is . . .
W: Why this is important is because . . .
N: Some next steps include . . .

Reflect on the outcome. What else will you do to be effective giving redirecting feedback? What strategies will you implement to reinforce the behavioral change, to help them reach the desired modifications through your coaching?

Continue to use OWN to help create a feedback culture and establish the foundation for additional coaching.

3. How does your leader coach style (Analytical, Results, People, Thought) impact how you give feedback? What do you do well? Where do you want to improve? What are some strategies you will put in place to be more consistent giving feedback?

Go to www.thesagealliance.com/worksheets to download the following worksheet that will help you chart your progress.

OWN for Giving Feedback

sage alliance

Observations → Why → Next Steps

Select a positive, reinforcing example to provide feedback. Use OWN to plan your conversation.

Observations: _____

_____

Why (the Impact): _____

_____

Next Steps: _____

_____

Select a corrective, redirecting example to provide feedback. Use OWN to plan your conversation.

Observations: _____

_____

Why (the Impact): _____

_____

Next Steps: _____

_____

© Sage Alliance 2019   www.thesagealliance.com

Go Slower to Go Faster

Sometimes you have to go slower to go faster. Taking the time now to help an employee develop critical problem-solving techniques results in going faster in the future. Your objective is to not only solve today's challenges, it is to solve tomorrow's challenges as well.

You now have an acute understanding of what it means to be a leader coach and leverage the SAGE Coaching Approach with your team. Now is the time to put this into action. Be intentional and identify the behaviors you need to address to be an effective leader coach. Your commitment to do this now will ensure you build a high-performing team as you continue to develop your own leadership skills.

Be Intentional

You consider yourself a manager who successfully executes on your initiatives and the priorities expected of you. Admirable, but building a high-performing team requires you to slow down and reflect on how to accomplish your goals in parallel with developing your team. It's easy to let the fast pace derail you from spending the needed time to coach.

There are always fires that need extinguishing or imminent deadlines that need to be met. You need to consciously and deliberately commit to take the actions that will help you effectively coach your team. Only then can they learn how to be better leaders themselves and grow their leadership footprint.

Be intentional in each of the following competencies to raise your leadership to the leader coach level:

- Listen Actively
- Express Curiosity
- Practice Patience
- Stay Focused
- Delegate Authority
- Encourage Authentically
- Support Failing Safely

Your ability to hone each of these attributes will help you be a great leader coach.

Your Field Guide

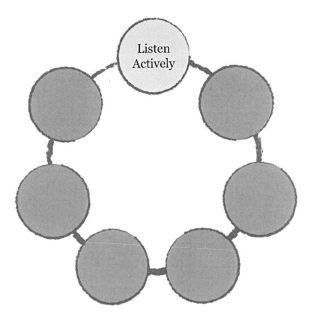

A lot has been written about active listening as an important leadership attribute and key tenet of successful coaching. Think back to a time your employee asked you something and you began nodding your head, maybe even putting your hand up to stop them from speaking. As you gazed at them with a satisfied smile, you instinctively replied to their request, without waiting for them to finish. You knew how to help them, maybe even had experienced the same challenge, and wanted to offer your counsel. But that is not active listening.

Author Stephen R. Covey said, "Most people do not listen with the intent to understand; they listen with the intent to reply."[1] I take this idiom one step further. Most leaders do not listen with the intent to understand; they listen with the intent to *find a solution.*

When someone approaches you with a challenge, you immediately go into solution mode and figure out how you can help them solve that challenge. Unfortunately, you have stopped listening to some important cues that will help you be a better leader coach.

In the SAGE Coaching Approach, listening actively is a key behavior to provide fundamental information. Listening will inform you of where the employee is struggling and allow you a better understanding of the challenges they are facing. By listening actively, you take in more information to help you guide the employee to problem resolution. The emphasis is on helping the employee solve the problem instead of you automatically providing them with the answer and *solutioning* for them.

Acknowledge: The best way to leverage active listening is to be fully engaged and listen to the employee. Acknowledging sends a message that you are listening. It shows you recognize what the employee is saying is important and indicates an appreciation for where they may falter. This can be demonstrated with a simple statement, such as, "I recognize this isn't an easy task." The employee will be more open to your coaching when you demonstrate you understand their challenge through acknowledgment.

Summarize and Rephrase: Summarizing what you heard ensures understanding, yours and theirs. This is especially true if the employee is having trouble gathering their thoughts and communicating them in a concise manner. There are times when you need to rephrase what was said. Rephrasing can help when you need clarity on what the employee is trying to communicate.

A simple way to do this is to say, "What I hear you saying is . . ." Then restate what you believe the employee has communicated. The employee will either agree with your understanding or provide additional commentary. Rephrasing what they said can shed new light to help you determine the next steps for coaching. A great indicator that you, in fact, understand what the employee has said is when they say something like, "Yes, that's exactly what I'm saying." With that, trust is built, the employee develops an appreciation for your approach, and the coaching progresses further.

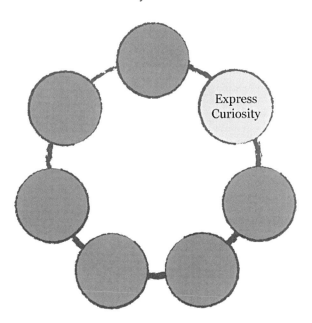

Along with active listening, expressing curiosity is the single biggest skill for being a great leader coach. Think back to when you were a child and you were fascinated with everything around you. You asked questions to gather more information and make connections between one thing and another. If you have children in your life, you probably hear them ask the darndest questions. This demonstrates their curiosity about things they do not understand or want to know more about.

Imagine connecting with your inner child and getting curious about the situations that challenge your employees. When you ask questions, this can prompt them to look at circumstances from a different perspective. Practice letting yourself drift back to when you were a child and ask curious questions, not for the sake of uncovering facts, data, and details, but rather to explore additional alternatives with the employee.

Ask Thought-Provoking Questions: Asking inquisitive or thought-provoking questions enables you to channel your curiosity. Use these at any time in the SAGE Coaching Approach. They are especially helpful when the employee is stuck or unsure of what to do next. This enables the employee to reflect and look at the situation from a different perspective.

Examples of thought-provoking questions include:

- How do you see the situation?
- What is your assessment of this situation?
- In a perfect world, how would you like it to be?
- What is your vision for this?
- What have you thought about doing?
- What is stopping you from moving forward?
- What if you do nothing?

Ask Open-Ended Questions: What do all of these questions have in common? They are open-ended. They are not simple yes-or-no questions, but multifaceted ones. They cause the responder to think and reflect before answering. As a result of asking open-ended questions, you will get a wealth of information about the situation, the employee, and the challenges they are facing.

Open-ended questions provide the employee with a blueprint for things to consider when they encounter a similar situation in the future. Employees learn to exercise critical thinking and consider different perspectives for solving a problem or exploring implications for various alternatives. You are modeling the SAGE Coaching Approach while you are helping the employee to solve problems themselves.

I see leaders struggle with asking open-ended questions. It is easy to say, "Seems like you're struggling here; is that true?" To which the reply is "Yes" or "No." From this interaction, your immediately solving the problem becomes the next logical step. But this is not the SAGE Coaching Approach.

Instead ask, "What is your assessment of this situation?" With this question, you receive invaluable information that goes beyond the simple yes or no to understand the employee's challenges. You discover the reason *why* they are struggling instead of confirming something you already know.

Of course, there is a place for close-ended questions. For example, you can use close-ended questions to confirm a piece of information or verify the accuracy of a situation. However, in the SAGE Coaching Approach, open-ended questions are far more powerful and give you an abundance of information to coach the employee.

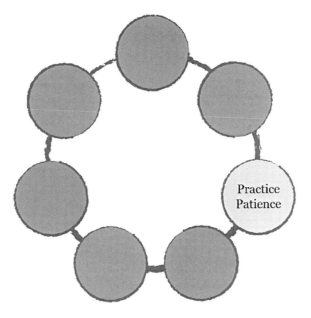

Patience empowers your team to take the needed time to figure out a tough problem. To be successful, you must suspend judgment and shift your focus from the need for immediate results, which can be a challenge with the rapid pace within your organization.

Slowing down to coach may test your patience. You pride yourself on being able to move mountains to achieve the impossible. Yet impatience can arise when you feel like you know the answer, but your employee is not connecting the dots as quickly, or arriving at the same solution. With your bias for action, you may find you perform the task yourself or tell your team how to complete it.

Sometimes you have to go slower to go faster. Taking the time now to help an employee develop critical problem-solving techniques results in going faster in the future. Your objective is to not only solve today's challenges, it is to solve tomorrow's challenges as well. You will reap the benefits when the employee is able, through trial and error, to make better decisions, without your continuous intervention. Your patience promotes learning, improves satisfaction, boosts confidence, and motivates the team.

Active listening and asking questions are the key tenets for not only managing impatience but for being a leader coach. Your time investment will pay off enormously. Patience establishes your commitment to the employee to develop them further.

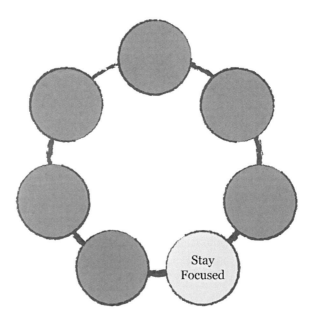

In the twenty-four/seven world we live in, it is commonplace to multitask. An employee comes into your office and you continue writing your email while listening to what they say. But are you really engaged?

Research shows there is no such thing as multitasking. In fact, those who think they are the best at multitasking are the worst at doing more than one thing at a time. Take a look at an everyday activity like driving. If you just layer on one more thing, such as listening to the radio, the amount of attention or brain bandwidth going toward driving decreases by about 37 percent.[2] Consequently, you are not multitasking. You have in fact reduced the amount of attention you are now paying to your driving.

You cannot do two tasks at the same level of expertise at the same time. One task is eventually going to suffer. Imagine someone reading their text messages as they walk along the street. (I know you are grinning, as I am, thinking of this image.) I have seen people fall off the sidewalk, trip over a crack in the road, walk into a pole, or worse, walk into oncoming traffic.

As such, you may find yourself becoming preoccupied with a deadline, checking the time to ensure you are not late to an upcoming meeting, or scrutinizing your phone over a text message while an employee is in your office. A leader coach knows the importance of staying focused.

Instead, listen and observe. In this way you pick up the cues, both verbal and nonverbal, the employee is displaying that will help you coach them. When you are engaged, you instinctively perceive things that are not explicitly said. It may be the employee's facial expression, body language, or tone of voice that will communicate how they are feeling or whether they are committed to the course of action. When you stay in the moment and remain focused, you pick up additional information that will help you be an effective leader coach.

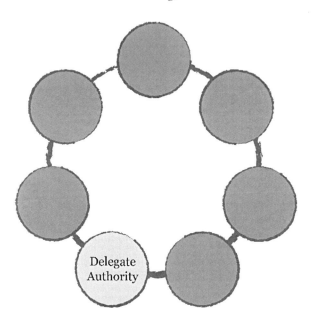

There is no shortage of work to be completed, but to be effective as a leader coach, you must entrust your team to do the job they commit to do. You may not even realize you are micromanaging since you have a stake in the outcome. You see this as your span of control, staying on top of everything to drive the strategic direction. It is natural for you to be involved in problem solving and decision making. After all, you are ultimately accountable for the success or failure of a given initiative.

To be an effective leader coach, you need to let go of control and allow your team to take ownership of key initiatives. Collaboratively uncover the root cause, including any roadblocks and challenges the employee may encounter. Communicate expectations up front and agree on deadlines. Coach your employees to develop plans, strategies, and tactics and assure them you are available should they encounter any complications.

This ensures you will feel more at ease that the work is getting done, and you will be alerted to potential delays or other necessary updates. Delegating in this way establishes ownership and accountability among your team, and enables you to step back from micromanaging and focus on the more important things like coaching your team.

When you do this successfully, your employees see you trust them, have confidence in their abilities, and value their judgment. Ultimately, delegating authority develops your team and prepares them to innovate and make autonomous decisions, even when they reach an obstacle.

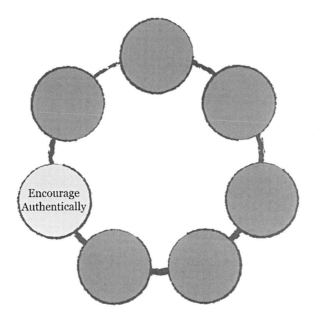

There are times your employees may feel overwhelmed or uncertain of the course of action. Or you discern they do not have the confidence to make a tough decision. This is where encouragement is critical. Encouragement can sometimes be the impetus an employee needs to overcome an obstacle.

Encourage the employee by letting them know you appreciate their hard work and you believe in their ability to accomplish their goals. In nearly every case, it helps them feel more confident and optimistic. Encouragement can be demonstrated simply by acknowledging that what they are working on is challenging. Encourage them by saying, "I know you can do it." This simple statement can be a defining moment in helping the employee persevere.

I call this authentic encouragement because it comes from the heart. Many leaders struggle giving positive feedback when what they requested the employee to undertake is expected as part of their job. However, this does not recognize the effort it took, the obstacles they overcame, or the soft skills they employed like building rapport and establishing trust.

Encouraging authentically validates that they are heading in the right direction and reinforces future positive behaviors. When you encourage, you inspire and motivate the employee to achieve more and believe they can succeed. But this has to be genuine and authentic for your leadership style.

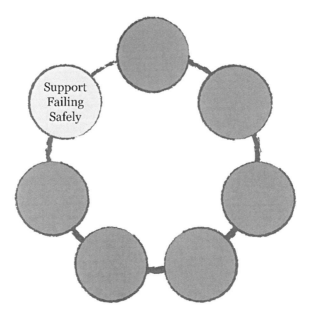

Using the SAGE Coaching Approach inherently supports the employee in making tough decisions by encouraging them to take risks and explore the unknown. When employees know you have their best interests at heart and you trust their judgment, they are more confident in leading, executing, and owning the result, even if the decision they arrive at goes awry. There is a blind faith you must demonstrate that supports the employee in taking risks and failing safely.

This is not to say you will encourage or allow them to make a catastrophic mistake. Rather, you create a safe place where they can try new ideas and approaches and, with you as their guide, steer clear of the precipice.

When you move away from finding the right answer and telling the employee how to complete a task, this creates space for them to explore new opportunities. The employee is willing to try something new or do something differently than you would. The employee will learn from the obstacles they face and, when necessary, will learn how to rebound when they fail. As a leader coach, you help the employee grow and develop further by providing this safe space.

Take the time to show the employee you are interested and invested in them. This empowers the employee to stretch out of their comfort zone as they try new things. While they may have stumbled, being supportive helps build their confidence to persevere, take the necessary risks, and try new approaches.

As a result, you inspire them to continue to learn, to be challenged, and to develop their own leadership skills. Additional coaching will help them uncover areas where they were effective and areas where they were less effective, and pinpoint future approaches that will lead to success.

Your Call to Action

Reflections I Will Make

In which of the following areas will you commit to develop your coaching approach?

- ☐ Listen Actively
- ☐ Express Curiosity
  - ○ Ask Thought-Provoking Questions
  - ○ Ask Open-Ended Questions
- ☐ Practice Patience
- ☐ Stay Focused
- ☐ Delegate Authority
- ☐ Encourage Authentically
- ☐ Support Failing Safely

Actions I Will Take

1. Jot down a few thought-provoking questions that you can have at the ready when you feel yourself slipping into advising. Get curious! Craft at least three that will help you master asking open-ended questions. Leverage these questions to uncover where an employee is struggling or where they may not be as committed as you previously thought to make a decision or take action.

2. Think about an example of when you became impatient with one of your employees. What caused you to feel this way? Were they not connecting the dots, or not making progress quickly enough, or something else? What are some strategies that will help you practice patience? Write down three actions you will take to stay in the moment, stay focused, and be patient.

3. Identify at least one employee with whom you have established enough mutual trust that you can let them fail safely. Your support will help them try a new approach to solve an upcoming challenge. You may know a better way to complete the task successfully; however, you are going to put your faith in this employee and allow them to try something different.

Remember, provide encouragement along the way so they remain steadfast. How did it go? What did you learn about your leader coach style (Analytical, Results, People, Thought)? What strengths and cautions did you see emerge when you delegated authority and ownership? What will you do differently in the future to ensure success?

Go to www.thesagealliance.com/worksheets to download the following worksheet that will help you chart your progress.

---

sage alliance

Coaching Cautions Self-Assessment

Check the appropriate option to indicate how consistently you demonstrate each of these behaviors.

		Rarely	Sometimes	Often
1.	Listening Actively			
2.	Express Curiosity			
3.	Practice Patience			
4.	Stay Focused			
5.	Delegate Authority			
6.	Encourage Authentically			
7.	Support Failing Safely			

What strategies will you implement to be effective in each of the areas identified for improvement?

_____

_____

_____

www.thesagealliance.com

Leader Coach, Beware

Knowing what to do to empower autonomy, stimulate decisiveness, and instill confidence in your employees can help you grow in your role. Knowing what not to do can save you time and frustration, get your team on track and feeling confident, and allow you to address more far-reaching matters that need your attention.

Through reading this book and learning the SAGE Coaching Approach, you now know what coaching is and what it is not. And you know how to apply effective coaching behaviors to your role as a leader, transforming you into a leader coach. You have learned this new approach, but have you thought about the impediments that can get in the way of being the most effective leader coach?

Your mindset might still be fixed on driving the ultimate outcome for your team. Perhaps you have been in a leadership position for so long, "doing" leadership the same way and getting satisfactory results, that you find it difficult to adopt a new approach. At the same time, you know that to improve results you have to do something different. For you to truly be successful in the long term and make the transformation you desire, you must look at things differently.

It's Not about You

Being a leader coach requires you to get out of the way. This might sound harsh, but coaching is not about you; it's about the needs of the person you are coaching. Remember, one of your primary goals as a leader coach is to develop your employees into confident, empowered leaders themselves. You cannot do that unless you focus on their needs.

This does not mean you have no concerns for the organization's bottom line, your own career growth, or customer satisfaction. In fact, each of these stakeholders benefits when you focus on the employee's needs. And you can only do that when you get out of the way. So, what does it mean to get out of the way?

Turn your attention to the employee you are coaching and determine what they need to be more effective and take responsibility for the outcomes. Being adept at leveraging each of these competencies is what helps you uncover the employee's need.

Your ability to collaboratively uncover where the employee needs assistance ensures you are coaching to their true challenge. Remember, it is not always where the employee thinks they need help. Instead, you may conclude the employee has difficulty making tough decisions, lacks confidence, shies away from conflict, or something else entirely. Once you identify this, the rest of the process unfolds seamlessly. With a clear understanding of the employee's need, you will be on the road to transform from leader to leader coach. Refer to chapter 9 for how to leverage each of these seven attributes to uncover and coach the employee's need.

We have discussed cautions at each step in the SAGE Coaching Approach; however, now we are taking a deeper dive to hone your coaching skills to a finer point. You must be intentional. Practice, redirect, and correct to avoid these pitfalls and become accomplished in leader coaching.

Caution: Watch Your Step

Knowing what to do to empower autonomy, stimulate decisiveness, and instill confidence in your employees can help you grow in your role. Knowing what not to do can save you time and frustration, get your team on track and feeling confident, and allow you to address more far-reaching matters that need your attention.

Consider the following behaviors to avoid as you practice the SAGE Coaching Approach:

⌁ Advising, Telling, or Instructing
⌁ Asking "Why" Questions
⌁ Framing Suggestions as Questions
⌁ Overlooking the Root Cause
⌁ Quick Fixes
⌁ Providing Too Few Options
⌁ Jumping into Solution Mode
⌁ Being Vague and Not Actionable
⌁ Disregarding Accountability

As a leader with deep experience solving many issues, it is natural for you to advise the employee on how to manage the situation. You have been faced with the same or similar challenges and you have the experience of handling these and solving them. And you want to save the employee from stumbling, or worse, failing.

You may also find you fall back into a telling approach when you are under pressure or time constraints. When you advise, tell, or instruct, you do not give the employee the opportunity to come up with a solution on their own. They will forever rely on you to be the hero or heroine who solves their problems.

Move from telling and advising to exploring options. When you do this, you will naturally move into the SAGE Coaching Approach. Ask some of the questions we reviewed in prior chapters to help the employee move to an advantageous solution without instructing or giving them advice.

Avoid questions that start with "why." Why, you might ask? *Why* questions can often seem like you are questioning the employee and their rationale, putting them on the defensive. They feel like they must defend their position and justify their responses, whether they feel the actions are correct or not.

Think of some common *why* questions you ask. These may seem innocuous to you, but the employee may feel like you are interrogating them, or worse, you do not trust their judgment. Therefore, you and the employee may never get to the actual solution or the true answer.

Here are examples of common *why* questions to avoid and suggestions to rephrase these questions into *what* questions.

Why	What
Why are you doing that?	What steps did you take in this situation?
Why did you do that?	What is driving you to take this action(s)?
Why did you say that?	What is prompting you to say this?
Why do you think that is a good solution?	What criteria did you use to evaluate this solution? OR What other solutions have you considered?

When you ask *what* questions, you gain additional information about the situation and the approach the employee took. This is invaluable in helping the employee solve the issue independently. Another option is to respond with "Tell me more." This open-ended statement can prompt the employee to provide useful information that will help in getting them back on track.

Asking questions that start with "have you" is another instance where you think you're coaching but you're not. Although this is framed as a question, this is suggestive and does not allow the employee to come up with the solution on their own.

Examples of suggestive questions include:

- Have you thought of this?
- Have you done this?
- Have you talked to . . .?

In reality, these are statements that are formed as questions. They are directives that imply *"Go do this."* The effect of this is threefold:

1. Shuts down brainstorming
2. Puts you as the leader in the expert advisor role
3. Negatively impacts ownership and accountability

You are merely leading an employee down a predetermined path. It may be hard for the employee to refuse your advice and say no, even if they do not believe it is a good option. What happens next is that ownership plunges to zero. The employee has not bought into the solution and does not see this as something to pursue, so they don't.

Similarly, they may agree to pursue the option but pursue it half-heartedly. The employee does what they are *told*. They are not thinking for themselves and coming up with the solution independently. This will lead to less than stellar results. Your goal is to empower the employee to come up with the answers independently, with your guidance. If you continue to suggest or advise, you're not coaching, and you're not empowering the employee.

You can rephrase *have you* questions into *what* or *who* questions. Suggestions include:

- What alternatives have you thought of?
- What options do you want to explore?
- What steps did you take?
- What steps make sense here?
- Who else can help you with this challenge?

This puts the employee back in the driver's seat by empowering them to think through the challenges and arrive at a solution. Now you are in a position to coach them on where they need your help, not necessarily on what you surmised before you engaged your curiosity.

This is one of the greatest risks I see. All too often, leaders coach on a particular detail, but not on the underlying cause. Without understanding this, it is virtually impossible to help the employee improve in this area without knowing what is really standing in the way.

As an example, if someone is not delegating, it could be they fear losing control, or they think they can do it better than anyone else, or they are unable to prioritize. Therefore, they are holding on to work they could otherwise delegate. You coach the employee differently if it is about fear of losing control versus their inability to prioritize. Getting curious and asking open-ended, thought-provoking questions will help you uncover the root cause.

As humans, there is a natural tendency to try to fix a situation. You want to fix something that is broken, especially when you have the expertise to do so. If something needs to get done quickly, you tell yourself it is easier to do it yourself and commit to coach at a later date when you have the luxury of more time. But the next pressing matter inevitably renders coaching elusive.

We live in a twenty-four/seven world where almost instantaneous response is expected, and you think you must always have a solution at the ready. Unfortunately, this is like putting a bandage on a broken limb. By doing something, you feel better. But the quick fix does not solve the longer-term issue. Instead, strive for the higher learning that a coaching approach affords. The simple, quick fix may be a good solution, but it does not develop your team to solve tough challenges and remove obstacles on their own.

You may wonder why you would continue to brainstorm when the employee has found the answer. The answer is simple. If you think of your interactions with employees as an opportunity to coach, you will want to go beyond finding the single, right answer. Instead, brainstorming teaches the employee useful skills in problem solving and decision making.

While providing too few options is the larger concern, some leaders love a good brainstorm and continue with questioning even after the employee has confidently arrived at a solution. If you are this leader, make sure the coaching session is not an exercise in futility. The ultimate goal is to identify enough options that help the employee explore creative yet actionable ways to solve a problem.

Finding the right number of options is not a science. Generate as many as you can, typically more than three. To do this, leverage your and your employees' creative thinking. You might be surprised and uncover something you haven't thought of.

If, during your coaching, you ask the employee to think of some options to solve the issue, or you ask them what they think they should do and they reply with *"I don't know,"* you might feel compelled to furnish the answer yourself. In all likelihood, you know the answer and you want to help the employee arrive at the same conclusion.

When you are tempted to jump in and solve the problem for them, consider this. You are depriving them of an opportunity to develop, make tough decisions, and learn to take calculated risks when faced with ambiguity or uncertainty.

When an employee asks you what they should do in a particular situation and you respond with "What do you think you should do?", you are at a fork in the decision tree. At this point, they might answer with some options, but invariably they will say something to the effect of "If I knew what to do, I would not be asking you."

Regrettably, you will take this at face value and shift directly into solution mode instead of offering to brainstorm solutions with them. This *is* an opportunity to coach.

Many people fall into this trap and think "doing more" is an actionable goal. As an example, if the agreement is to delegate more, while this is a positive goal, it is not specific or actionable. To delegate five times over the next week is specific. Even more specific is to identify the five tasks or initiatives to delegate over the next week.

The more specificity, the more actionable the goal will be. When the goal is actionable, the employee has greater chance at success. Guard against having a great coaching conversation without ensuring the goal is specific and actionable. For further questions you can leverage to make the goal actionable, refer to chapter 6 on the Goal-Setting step in the SAGE Coaching Approach.

I have observed countless interactions between managers and employees, and surprisingly, accountability is not always clearly stated. The leader and employee may have a good conversation, but the commitments and the ramifications for not achieving these commitments may not be clear. The ramifications are based on the impact for doing or not doing a particular action.

If a deadline is missed, the impact may be missing a customer commitment or people losing faith in an employee's ability to do what they say. Or it may cause additional work for the team, for certain team members, or for you as the leader. When there is clarity around accountability, all parties understand the implications if an action is dropped or not followed through. Asking specific questions in the Execution and Accountability step of the SAGE Coaching Approach will help here. Refer to chapter 7 for additional questions to establish sustainable accountability.

Leaders at all levels must commit to putting in the needed time to coach, empower, and engage their team. Sometimes you have to slow down in order to move faster. The time you invest in coaching will help you do just that. By taking the time to coach up front, you will have more time in the long run as you see your team become more decisive and solve problems on their own.

Your Call to Action

Reflections I Will Make

Of these top nine cautions, which area do you want to work on most? Check the box for each that applies to you.

☐ Advising, Telling, or Instructing
☐ Asking "Why" Questions
☐ Framing Suggestions as Questions
☐ Overlooking the Root Cause
☐ Quick Fixes
☐ Providing Too Few Options
☐ Jumping into Solution Mode
☐ Being Vague and Not Actionable
☐ Disregarding Accountability

Actions I Will Take

1. Moving from *why* to *what*. Keep a log. Write down every time you use a *why* question over the next month. Reword each of these into *what* questions and practice them every chance you get. Check your log and review your progress. Are you using fewer *why* questions?

2. Rephrase *have you* questions to *what* questions. Keep a log and review regularly to chart your progress for omitting these questions from your vocabulary.

3. Be on the lookout for an opportunity when an employee says, "I don't know." This is an ideal time to explore whether they are lacking knowledge, experience, or confidence, or see whether they fear they will look foolish and damage their reputation. Once

you determine their concern, this is a perfect opportunity to coach based on the challenge you uncover. How can you leverage your leader coach style (Analytical, Results, People, Thought) to help them be successful? What cautions do you need to be aware of that will impede success? What strategies will you employ to be successful?

Go to www.thesagealliance.com/worksheets to download the following worksheet that will help you chart your progress.

sage
alliance

Ask Open-Ended Questions

Moving from *Why* to *What*
Keep a log of every time you use a *why* question. Reword each of these into *what* questions.

Date	Why?	What?

Rephrase *Have you* questions to *What* questions
Keep a log and review regularly to chart your progress for rewording these questions.

Date	Have You . . .?	What?

© Sage Alliance 2019   www.thesagealliance.com

You're Surrounded (by Coaching Opportunities)!

Coaching is not something you have to find time for. Coaching is the foundation of who you are as a leader. This is not something you add to your endless list of priorities. Coaching should be done every day, in every interaction, and in countless scenarios.

I have had the pleasure of working with many leaders in my coaching practice and through my workshops, and they all share a common hurdle: finding the time to coach. These leaders aren't coaching, because of their demanding schedules and tight deadlines. Like you, they must balance a heavy workload, respond to urgent matters, and manage their teams. We all get busy. We all have deadlines. And we all have responsibilities as leaders, one of which is to lead and coach while executing on our priorities.

Don't Miss These: Five Scenarios to Coach

Coaching is not something to do sometime in the future. Lack of time is a poor excuse, and it is a sure path to failure. Ironically, coaching is not something you have to find time for. Coaching is the foundation of who you are as a leader. This is not something you add to your endless list of priorities. Coaching should be done every day, in every interaction, and in countless scenarios.

Anytime an employee asks for help, you have an opportunity to coach. You must adopt the mindset that coaching is not a task you check off on your mounting to-do list. In fact, coaching *is* leadership, and you should be coaching every day.

Coaching is an opportunity to empower your employees and equip them with the skills to be better leaders. It is an opportunity to facilitate engagement, problem solving, decision making, ownership, and accountability. Most situations are coachable and therefore offer you the opportunity to coach. But if you do not recognize a situation as a coaching opportunity, you can certainly miss it.

Here are five scenarios when you should coach, even though you may think otherwise.

1. Lacks expertise. If someone needs further training or simply does not know how to complete a task, they are going to need your expert advice to point them in the right direction. This is where you, as the manager, need to identify what assistance they need through the Situation Analysis phase of the SAGE Coaching Approach. This may warrant further training, shadowing another employee, or something else entirely to gain the needed knowledge or expertise. Together, you and the employee will develop a plan.

When you leverage the SAGE Coaching Approach, you will help this employee work on developing their skills further in the targeted area. Together you agree on a goal around gaining the needed expertise. This may take the shape of what they are going to do or whom they need to work with and the time frame for which they want to achieve this.

Your coaching will center around helping them take ownership, be accountable, and complete the steps to reach the identified goal. In this instance, be sure to focus on when there is truly a lack of skill. Do not confuse this with someone who has the expertise but may lack confidence or be afraid to make a tough decision.

2. New to a position or company. Similar to learning a new skill, if someone is new to a position, role, or company, they may not know the process, procedures, or personnel who can help them reach their goal. As any good manager knows, this is a time when you have to teach, instruct, or advise.

As the employee gets up to speed, you should coach them to stay on course and remain accountable. Work together to set up goals for when they should be at a particular knowledge level, or to develop the plan around a specific goal or level of mastery. Coach them around taking ownership and remaining accountable to the goal or plan.

I have always been a fan of developing a 30-60-90-day plan when an employee is new. I would typically ask the employee to put the parameters together, and then I would suggest considerations I thought were missing.

This approach ensures they buy in to the plan since it is of their own making. Then focus your efforts on coaching them to achieve the plan. A great coaching question you can leverage here is, "On a scale of one to ten, how likely are you to follow through with this plan?"

3. Only one answer. There are times when there is only one answer to a problem. How much is two plus two? When an employee responds with "I don't know," they do not have the information to solve the problem, or they may not be aware of the process or procedure. Coaching an employee on two plus two is controlling and can cause frustration for all concerned. Instead of leading them with questions such as "Have you thought about two plus two equaling four?", provide them with the necessary information, and then you can begin coaching.

You can coach them on how to implement the process and remain accountable in leveraging their newfound knowledge. Coach them on how to identify trusted resources and subject matter experts who can assist when they are confused or uncertain about a process. Learning happens over time, and your coaching ensures they continue to gain the necessary expertise and implement a process for continuous learning.

4. In an emergency. If you were to discover a fire in your office building, and survival was paramount, it would not be the right time to explore options and weigh pros and cons. It is time to find the nearest exit and get everyone out safely.

By the same token, there may be a request that comes from high up in the organization or from the board that seems like an emergency. In today's culture, it is easy to treat everything as an emergency and not coach when you should. You must decide what constitutes an emergency and act accordingly. Resist using "emergency" as a scapegoat for avoiding coaching opportunities. Make coaching a priority, and you will find that what you once thought of as an emergency will become less so.

5. Lacks confidence. When an employee comes to you for help to solve a problem, they likely know what to do but may lack the confidence to do it themselves. Unless you know they truly lack knowledge or expertise, deem them capable of solving the problem and challenging themselves—with your support, of course.

Rather than give in to your natural inclination to problem-solve, ask, "What do *you* think you should do?"

I have heard many employees respond with, "I wouldn't be coming to you if I knew the answer." In reality, they do know the answer, but most often they do not have the confidence to pursue the solution given the visibility of the project or the complexity of the situation. This exposes an additional avenue to coach. Ask the employee if they would like to brainstorm some options. The next place you can explore is by asking one of these questions:

- ⁓ What have you already tried?
- ⁓ What have you done in similar situations?
- ⁓ What are some other perspectives?
- ⁓ What obstacles are standing in your way?
- ⁓ What is preventing you from choosing a course of action?

All five of these questions stimulate conversation and encourage the employee to reflect, assess, and use critical thinking to generate ideas to move closer to a solution.

You will find they have at least one idea, most likely multiple, of what can or cannot work. If, in fact, the options they already tried did not work, explore why they failed and come up with options that will achieve the desired results. The crux of this is for you to avoid filling the void with the solution, and instead use the SAGE Coaching Approach to facilitate the conversation to help them come up with the answer.

As you can see, coaching is pervasive. Although there may be times when you must manage first, there is always an opportunity to coach. There are an infinite number of reasons to coach that include career discussions, problem solving, development opportunities, obstacles, changes or conflicts, misunderstandings between employees, and so on.

Using another approach in your leadership arsenal, like conveying knowledge, should not prevent you from using the SAGE Coaching Approach in parallel. Every moment lends itself to a coaching approach.

Make the Most of One-on-Ones

Coaching requires you to be intentional. One of the most proactive ways to do that is to schedule regular one-on-one meetings with each of your team members. This ensures you are spending the time with each employee and coaching them to accomplish their goals.

This is not a status update where employees share their step-by-step progress on a specific task or initiative. Rather, it is an opportunity for you to coach the employee. During this meeting, you will help them develop the specific skill set to aid them in overcoming an obstacle, reaching a specified milestone, identifying issues and solutions, or achieving a career goal.

The frequency of these meetings is completely up to you. Consider biweekly or monthly one-on-ones to share what is working well and what areas need development. This will help you carve out time to coach and ensure it becomes part of your leader coach approach. You can combine this with existing one-on-ones. Be certain you devote enough time so the discussion is not solely focused on the progress and status of any one initiative, but on the employee and their development in reaching a positive outcome or career goal.

Make this a priority. Hold these often enough that you can keep a consistent flow while building on prior conversations. Don't let other priorities usurp these one-on-ones. If you have not already established this, your initial meeting should be centered around their career goals and areas that could stand in the way of the employee reaching their goals. Once this has been clearly identified, and you both agree on the areas of development, you need to prepare for future one-on-ones.

Envisioning how this meeting will go will help you be prepared and save you from falling into the usual trap of instructing and advising. Think through some of the thought-provoking, open-ended questions you want to ask. What do you need to know about this employee's career goals or areas they would like to develop? Your preparation will pay big dividends and allow you to intentionally practice the elements of the SAGE Coaching Approach.

I have included a worksheet you can use to help you prepare for your one-on-ones. You can download it at www.thesagealliance.com/worksheets.

Plant the Seeds and Watch Them Grow

As you think about your one-on-one meetings, a good place to start is assessing your team and determining the type of coaching each employee needs. Coaching is not a one-size-fits-all endeavor. Different employees need different types of support. Where they are in their career and development will determine the type of coaching you will need to deliver.

For a more focused coaching approach, use the Team Assessment Matrix to categorize your employees.

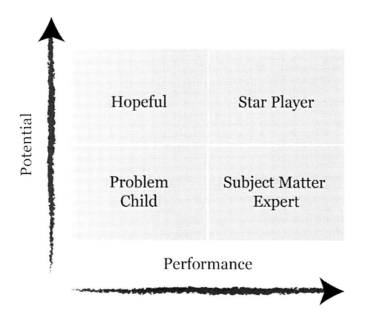

Problem Child

There is an array of reasons why you place someone in the Problem Child box. The common thread is they are not meeting performance expectations and they do not demonstrate further potential. This is someone who does not want to be promoted and may be happily focused on an explicit set of tasks and responsibilities. They are not motivated by promotions and, in all likelihood, do not want to put in the extra hours needed for advancement. More troubling is they have not demonstrated they have the skills to do what is required of them.

There is an opportunity to coach this employee, but you need to quickly determine their motivations to ascertain if coaching is worth your time. If not, then you need to think about how to manage them out of this role. Not everyone wants to be promoted. This is an opportunity to uncover positive contributions this employee can make by matching their skills to the right job.

I have seen examples over the years of situations where someone was put in a role they were not qualified for, and that they did not relish. Uncovering this can help you find the right place where this employee can contribute and add value. There are employees who want more time investment from their managers and didn't get this in previous situations.

Perhaps their job responsibilities were not the most visible or most critical, so they were left to their own devices with little direction or supervision. Over time, they realized their area of responsibility was not central to the organization, so they did as little as possible to get by. No one seemed to notice or care, or so they thought. They became reticent, and that bred mediocrity. The investment of time to coach this employee ultimately will benefit both the organization and the employee.

Coaching a Problem Child will center around uncovering their motivations and understanding what drives them. Examples of coaching questions include:

- What do you enjoy doing?
- What are you passionate about?
- What types of tasks bring your energy down?
- What type of work gives you energy?
- What would you like to do more of?
- What would you like to do less of?
- What's stopping you from performing at a higher level?
- What support do you need from me as your manager?

Subject Matter Expert

The Subject Matter Expert (SME) is a strong performer. Their deep knowledge can be leveraged to help others on the team gain additional insight and improve overall performance. The SME may have been with the organization for a long time, or they may be at a point in their career where they have put other priorities ahead of work, such as family or retirement. Therefore, moving up through the ranks of the company is not a priority for this employee.

Although they have little desire for promotion, they typically enjoy teaching others their area of expertise. They are consistent performers and the organization relies on their knowledge. Yet, sometimes managers become disinterested and apathetic with employees who are not striving for a promotion. The SME moves off your radar as a high potential, and you may not spend the needed time coaching them. There is, however, an opportunity to engage and empower them to ensure they know they are valued, which aids in their retention and continued performance.

A client of mine was placed in this box. She had younger children. Both she and her husband were employed and had agreed to pull back from upward mobility at work so they could focus on their growing family. The brief pause of her career advancement was essential for her. As her children matured, she refocused her attention on moving up in the organization. As a result, she shifted from an SME to a Star Player.

A small investment in an SME can pay enormous dividends. The first objective is to determine their career goal, which could be to either advance further in the company, to maintain their current position, or to engage in other, nonwork priorities, as mentioned earlier. Either way, you should coach this person, so they continue to feel valued as the go-to person in their area of expertise. This will ultimately serve the organization well.

Sample coaching questions to uncover their motivations include:

- What are your long-term aspirations?
- Where is your passion?
- How can I help you reach your longer-range goals?
- What do you like to do and how can I help you do more of this?

Hopeful

This employee is, by far, one of the best employees to coach.

They are motivated to succeed; nonetheless, their current capabilities are holding them back from making the contributions they are ultimately capable of. Hopefuls possess the ambition to perform as expected, even if they do not have years of experience or all the needed skills. They do, however, have the desire to learn. They are teachable, eager to please, and strive to learn new skills needed for their current role, as well as for advancement within the organization.

In most cases, the employee in the Hopeful quadrant falls into two possibilities: 1) They have not yet had the opportunity to learn new skills needed for their role, or 2) they may be in the wrong role. In either situation, they have yet to demonstrate first-rate performance. However, this presents the perfect coaching opportunity.

Sometime ago, I coached an employee who excelled in his role. As a result, he was promoted to a larger one. Unfortunately, the management team wrongly assumed he could pick up the larger role without any disruption. This caused my client to feel extreme dissatisfaction. He was constantly on edge to perform.

He realized the new position was not a good fit and consequently took a step back after only six months in the elevated role. It was the best decision he could have made. He was happier, began making contributions, and was once again seen as a top performer. The longer-range benefit was realized when another opportunity came along that he was better suited for. He was promoted and excelled in the new role.

Coaching someone in the Hopeful box needs to focus on the skills the employee needs to develop. Provide the needed training and allow time to bring them up to speed, then focus on creating a development plan to help this employee reach the desired goal. Coach them on setting clear goals and developing an action plan to remain on task and be accountable.

Sample coaching questions include:

- What will you do to acquire the needed skills?
- What is your plan to reach out to the people (we identified) who can help you get up to speed?
- When will you get started?
- How do you want to remain on task?
- What does success look like to you?

Star Player

Star Players are high-ambition and high-potential employees. They continually look for ways to learn and gain knowledge. They proactively seek new challenges and demonstrate interest in promotions. Wouldn't it be great to have a team of all Star Players? Maybe.

The risk with having too many Star Players on your team is attrition. They constantly need to be challenged and visible within the organization. If they feel they are being overlooked, or if further upward mobility is limited, they might seek opportunities elsewhere, triggering additional costs to hire and train their replacement.

Coaching a Star Player takes dedication on your part. They need to see you are investing in them and that you continue to give them challenging and high-visibility opportunities. Look for ways to stretch your Star Players. Many companies have programs where they identify high-potential employees and make a concerted effort to prepare these employees for the next steps in their careers. Regardless of whether your company has a formal program, the investment you make in coaching your Star Players has a significant return.

Leverage questions such as:

- Where do you see yourself in x years?
- What do you want to learn by being part of this initiative?

~ How can I best challenge you?
~ What would be a stretch goal for you?

Remember there are times when you may need to provide feedback before you can coach. Regardless of how you categorized your employees on potential and performance in the Team Assessment Matrix, they all need feedback, whether it is redirecting (corrective) or reinforcing (positive) behavior. Use the OWN Formula from chapter 8 to ensure you are optimizing your coaching by identifying when and where feedback is needed.

Use reinforcing feedback to highlight positive performance, encourage taking risks, empower employees, and build employees' self-confidence. Redirecting feedback needs to address underperformance, falling short of expectations, and skill-development deficits. When you provide feedback and follow this with coaching, you help employees understand what steps they need to take and the specific actions that will ensure success.

Download the Team Assessment Matrix to plot your team members and establish your coaching plan. You can download it here at www.thesagealliance.com/worksheets.

Your Call to Action

Reflections I Will Make

In which of these scenarios do you want to adopt a mindset to coach? Check all that apply.

- ☐ When expertise is lacking; to help seek additional knowledge
- ☐ When an employee is new to a position or to the company; to learn the ropes

☐ When there is only one answer; after sharing the necessary information

☐ When a situation seems like an emergency, but it is not

☐ When an employee lacks confidence

Action I Will Take

1. Assess where each of your employees is positioned in the Team Assessment Matrix and what specific coaching they require. Use the following steps to categorize them based on the different types of support they need:

   Step 1: Plot each employee, using the categories and descriptions for where you see their fit.

   Step 2: Prioritize employees based on degree of importance for coaching, in an effort to move them to a more advantageous position within the matrix.

   Step 3: Create a One-on-One Coaching Tracking form (see link at the end of the chapter) for each team member to prepare for your discussion. Develop your strategy, based on this worksheet, for each coaching discussion.

   Step 4: Schedule one-on-one meetings.

   Step 5: Set expectations for follow-up with the employee.

2. How will you flex your leader coach style (Analytical, Results, People, Thought) to best complement the employee you are coaching, given their placement in the Team Assessment Matrix?

3. What qualities of your leader coach style (Analytical, Results, People, Thought) will get in the way of you being successful?

Go to www.thesagealliance.com/worksheets to download the following worksheet that will help you chart your progress.

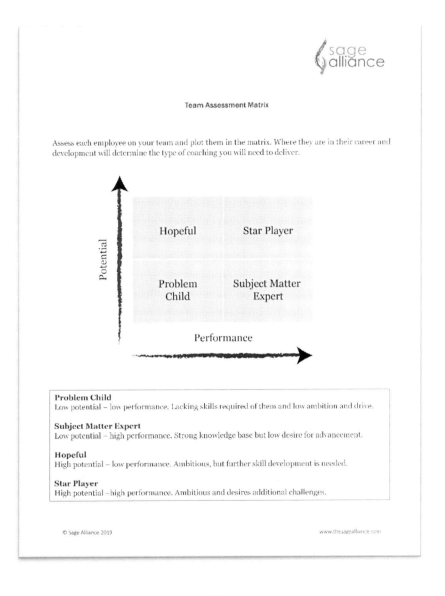

On Your Mark, Get Set, Go!

I am a big proponent of making activities tangible and actionable. It is not enough to read this book and nod your head along the way. It is time to put your plan into action. You need to determine what steps you will take to improve your coaching and transform from a leader into a leader coach using the SAGE Coaching Approach.

As you have learned in this book, coaching takes time, commitment, and practice. To help you remain accountable to the changes you want to make to transform into a leader coach, I have summarized the chapters and included an execution plan template for you to complete. It's time to get started. When will you implement the steps in the SAGE Coaching Approach? How often will you review your commitments, and how would you like to put them into practice?

The Big Leap

As a coach, I know one size does not fit all, and therefore the approach you take will be very different from someone else's. Now is the time for reflection. What works best for you when you want to incorporate a new approach or change a current one? Here are some suggestions of actions you can immediately take:

1. **Set reminders on your calendar.** I suggest a daily reminder at the start of each day to help you

frame your thinking around coaching. A weekly reminder at the end of the work week provides a time for reflection on your progress and the number of times you leveraged a coaching approach. Reviewing your progress helps you identify coaching opportunities for the upcoming week.

2. **Keep a tally.** Sometimes the simplest option is the best. To track your coaching progress, make two columns: the first is *Times I Coached*, and the second is *Missed Opportunities*. Keep this list handy and make a tick or notation in the appropriate column after every meeting and interaction with your team. This simple visual can be enough to acknowledge you need to move tick marks from the first column to the second in the upcoming days and weeks.

3. **Send an email recapping your coaching progress.** Yes, I am suggesting sending yourself an email, at a regularly scheduled day and time, each week. This is a great way to hold yourself accountable for coaching. This practice forces you to reflect as you recap your progress. This also reinforces your actions when it shows up in your own inbox for review.

4. **Enlist your team.** What better accountability than enlisting your team? Share your plan for working on modeling the SAGE Coaching Approach with your team. If they observe you telling, advising, or instructing (or any of the other coaching cautions), ask them to bring this to your attention.

5. **Identify an accountability partner.** Tell someone about your goals and ask them to hold you accountable. Choose someone who will be prepared to have the tough conversation if you do not do what you said you would. This can be a colleague, direct report, manager, significant other, friend, etc.

Your Call to Action

Reflections I Will Make

Now that you have a firm grasp of the SAGE Coaching Approach and the attributes that will make you most effective, think about what you have learned in this book and the exercises you have completed.

· Below is a summary of the areas we reviewed. Now that you have finished reading this book and learned how to be an effective leader coach, think about your takeaways. Check all the boxes that apply.

Chapter 1: You're Not Leading If You're Not Coaching
Roles I take when I think I'm coaching:

☐ Advisor
☐ Instructor
☐ Teacher
☐ Facilitator
☐ Boss
☐ Supervisor
☐ Manager

- ☐ Mentor
- ☐ Sounding Board
- ☐ Leader

Chapter 2: Transform from Manager to Leader Coach

- ☐ Analytical Leader
- ☐ Results Leader
- ☐ People Leader
- ☐ Thought Leader

Chapter 3: It's Time to Coach

- ☐ Situation Analysis
  - ↻ Clarify the challenges and obstacles
  - ↻ Ask questions to uncover the root cause
  - ↻ Listen and be curious
- ☐ Alternatives and Options
  - ↻ Brainstorm options
  - ↻ Weigh pros and cons
  - ↻ Encourage choosing the most advantageous option
- ☐ Goal Setting
  - ↻ Clarify goals
  - ↻ Gain alignment around goals and actions
  - ↻ Make goals actionable
- ☐ Execution and Accountability
  - ↻ Establish ownership
  - ↻ Build accountability
  - ↻ Provide encouragement and motivation

Chapter 4: Situation Analysis: Get Curious

- ☐ Ask more *who* questions
- ☐ Ask more *what* questions
- ☐ Ask more *where* questions
- ☐ Ask more *how* questions

Chapter 5: Alternatives and Options: The Good, the Bad, and the Shades in between

- ☐ Spend more time brainstorming alternatives and options
- ☐ Generate more than three options
- ☐ Weigh pros and cons
- ☐ Rank each option

Chapter 6: Goal Setting: Keep on Track

- ☐ Collaborate to establish clear goals with a positive outcome
- ☐ Set short-term goals to foster immediate action
- ☐ Assist with identifying long-term goals
- ☐ Assist with connecting short-term goals to (long-term) career goals

Chapter 7: Execution and Accountability: How Things Get Done

- ☐ Clarify ownership and accountability
- ☐ Specificity around measurements and milestones
- ☐ Facilitate an agreed-upon timeline to make it actionable
- ☐ Determine how committed the employee is to taking action
- ☐ Establish clear expectations for communications
- ☐ Offer encouragement and motivation

Chapter 8: The Feedback Loop

- ☐ Provide more positive, reinforcing feedback
- ☐ Identify opportunities to redirect behavior through corrective feedback
- ☐ Use OWN to get more comfortable and prepare for giving feedback
- ☐ Encourage team to provide you feedback using OWN
- ☐ Provide feedback to address behaviors and coach next steps so the employee knows how to proceed.

Chapter 9: Go Slower to Go Faster

- ☐ Listen Actively
- ☐ Express Curiosity
  - ○ Ask Thought-Provoking Questions
  - ○ Ask Open-Ended Questions
- ☐ Practice Patience
- ☐ Stay Focused
- ☐ Delegate Authority
- ☐ Encourage Authentically
- ☐ Support Failing Safely

Chapter 10: Leader Coach, Beware

- ☐ Advising, Telling, or Instructing
- ☐ Asking "Why" Questions
- ☐ Framing Suggestions as Questions
- ☐ Overlooking the Root Cause
- ☐ Quick Fixes
- ☐ Providing Too Few Options
- ☐ Jumping into Solution Mode
- ☐ Being Vague and Not Actionable
- ☐ Disregarding Accountability

Chapter 11: You're Surrounded (by Coaching Opportunities)!

- ☐ When expertise is lacking; to help seek additional knowledge
- ☐ When an employee is new to a position or to the company; to learn the ropes
- ☐ When there is only one answer; after sharing the necessary information
- ☐ When a situation seems like an emergency, but it is not
- ☐ When an employee lacks confidence

Actions I Will Take

1. Now that you know what it means to be a leader coach using the SAGE Coaching Approach, what will you do differently? Prioritize your top three takeaways from the checklist.

2. What are the steps you will take to make an immediate impact for you and your team? What strategies will you implement to be a great leader coach? Who can help you remain accountable and be successful in this endeavor?

3. As you think about all the opportunities for you to coach, what obstacles stand in the way of your success?

This starts today! It is your ongoing commitment to find the time to coach and make this part of your daily interactions with your team. Only then can you be a stronger leader coach.

My Execution Plan

Now is the time to make the commitment to coach. Fill in your personal execution plan in the template found here at www.the-sagealliance.com/worksheets. Set between three and five goals to help you be successful transforming into a leader coach. Refer to the six questions from chapter 6 to help you complete this plan.

Just Do It

Here is your chance to commit to adopting a new way of coaching your team and transforming into a leader coach. On a scale of 1–10, how likely are you to implement the steps you captured above? Circle the number below.

| 1 | 2 | 3 | 4 | 5 | 6 | 7 | 8 | 9 | 10 |

If this is not a 10, what needs to be in place for this to become a 10?

What specific steps will you take to move this to a 10?

You can do this!

Go to www.thesagealliance.com/worksheets to download the following worksheet that will help you chart your progress.

---

sage
alliance

My Execution Plan

Now is the time to make the commitment to coach. Fill in your personal execution plan in the template. Set between three and five goals to help you be successful transforming into a leader coach.

Goals
I will do the following . . .

1.

2.

3.

4.

5.

Desired Outcome
This is important because . . .
I will gain the following benefits . . .

1.

2.

3.

4.

5.

Key Steps
The specific steps I will take include . . .

1.

2

3.

4.

5.

Sage Alliance, Inc. 2019   www.thesagealliance.com

Overcoming Obstacles
What I will do when I encounter a roadblock . . .
Whom I will reach out to when I encounter a roadblock . . .

1.	
2.	
3.	
4.	
5.	

Time Frame
I will start this on . . .
I will finish this on . . .

1.	
2.	
3.	
4.	
5.	

Measures of Success
The following criteria will constitute my success . . .
The following people can provide feedback on my progress . . .

1.	
2.	
3.	
4.	
5.	

Acknowledgments

A heartfelt thanks to my family and friends for being great listeners. I have been talking about writing a book for more years than I care to recount.

A special thanks to Jason Allen, Maggie Bellville, Tricia Dempsey, Denise Harold, Dana Hughes, Helene Lollis, Dean Matthews, and Mary Welsh.

Thank you to all those who helped transform my manuscript into a book I can share with leaders: Anita Henderson, as well as the team at BookLogix.

A shout-out goes to the awesome people who provided their encouragement and great ideas. There are so many people who shared tips and their insight along my journey. If I overlooked mentioning your name, the mistake is all mine. I appreciate your input, and I took it all to heart. Thank you!

Now, as an author, I get to help a wide range of leaders transform into leader coaches. How great is that!

Endnotes

Introduction

1. Annamarie Mann and Jim Harter, "The Worldwide Employee Engagement Crisis," Gallup, January 7, 2016.

Chapter 1

1. 2017 International Coaches Federation (ICF) Global Consumer Awareness Study, PwC Research.
2. "Building a Coaching Culture with Millennial Leaders," Human Capital Institute (HCI) and the International Coaching Federation (ICF), 2017.
3. Allan Lee, Sara Willis, and Amy We Tian, "When Empowering Employees Works, and When It Doesn't," *Harvard Business Review*, March 2, 2018.
4. Joseph Folkman, "The 6 Key Secrets to Increasing Empowerment in Your Team," *Forbes*, March 2, 2017.
5. Mark Murphy, "Optimal Hours with the Boss" study, Leadership IQ, 2014.
6. Douglas Riddle, Emily R. Hoole, and Elizabeth C. D. Gullette, *The Center for Creative Leadership's Handbook of Coaching in Organizations* (San Francisco: John Wiley & Sons, 2015).
7. Hamish Knox, "The 4 Activities Leaders Should Spend the Majority of Their Time Doing," Sandler Training, January 5, 2016.

8. Jim Harter, "Employee Engagement on the Rise in the U.S.," Gallup, August 26, 2018.
9. Harter, "Employee Engagement on the Rise in the U.S."
10. Peter Drucker, management consultant and business author.

Chapter 2

1. "Building a Coaching Culture with Millennial Leaders," HCI and ICF.

Chapter 8

1. Jack Zenger and Joseph Folkman, "Your Employees Want the Negative Feedback You Hate to Give," *Harvard Business Review*, January 15, 2014.
2. "State of the American Manager: Analytics and Advice for Leaders," Gallup, 2017.

Chapter 9

1. Stephen Covey, *The 7 Habits of Highly Effective People: Powerful Lessons in Personal Change* (New York: Free Press, 2004).
2. Dr. Sanjay Gupta, "Your Brain on Multitasking," CNN, August 1, 2016.

About the Sage Alliance

Visit **www.thesagealliance.com** for additional resources and to learn firsthand how to become a great leader coach.

Keynote Speaking

Shelley speaks on leadership performance and team optimization to organizations, associations, and nonprofits. Whether it's a small gathering, keynote, conference, leadership retreat, association meeting, or women's organization, Shelley will customize a program based on your group's employee needs. Contact Shelley at speaking@thesagealliance.com.

Leadership Workshops

Sage Alliance, Inc. provides a series of customized workshops, both standalone and through the Leadership Academy, aimed at raising the high-potential funnel that becomes part of an organization's larger leadership initiatives. Sessions include:

- You Think You're Coaching, but You're Not: How Great Leaders Build High-Performing Teams
- The Power of Personal Branding: Making a Greater Impact as a Leader
- Breakthrough Communications
- Create a Lasting Impression: Commanding Communications and Persuasive Presence
- Identifying and Building Top Talent
- Dimensions of Delegation: The Secret to Leadership Success

~ Navigating the Maze of Change
~ Managing Conflict and Team Dynamics
~ Turning Your Vision into Goals
~ Zero In on Your Strengths: Grow Leadership through Increased Self-Awareness

Attendees leave with practical takeaways they can immediately implement to make an impact in their own leadership style, on their teams, and in their organizations.

Team Building

Sage Alliance, Inc. helps teams identify common goals, gain clarity around unclear roles, and uncover the successful dimensions to building and optimizing their teams. With an understanding of the roles within a team, communications will be improved, leading to increased collaboration as the team works toward a common goal. Industry-leading assessment tools are leveraged to help teams increase collaboration, develop a language for improved communication, and establish an approach for conflict resolution.

Executive Coaching

Sage Alliance, Inc. offers both individual and group coaching to help leaders prepare for the next stage in their career and make the necessary behavioral shifts that will help them be more successful. Industry-leading assessment tools are leveraged to help leaders gain insight into their strengths and opportunities for development.

Sage Alliance customizes one-to-one coaching programs to meet both employee and organizational needs. Top performers address growth opportunities and optimize their performance to reach their full potential. Leaders who are stepping into new roles, closing gaps, preparing for their next steps, and looking to make lasting change will benefit from the Sage Alliance coaching program.

The Sage Alliance group coaching program brings top performers in your organization together for continued development. High-potential leaders have the opportunity to interact with each other to gain additional awareness, collaborate, and build camaraderie within their peer group.

Group coaching helps leaders tackle mutual challenges, including increasing self-awareness, building talent, implementing succession planning, and expanding their influence. Leaders develop individual action plans and gain the benefit of group support to help achieve their goals.

Group coaching is a great way to extend the benefits of one-to-one coaching to a larger audience in a cost-effective manner.

Leadership Assessments

The following are the leadership assessments I use in my coaching and team building:

- Birkman Method
- DiSC
- Herrmann Brain Dominance Instrument (HBDI)
- Hogan Assessments

Worksheets and Tools

To download the worksheets and tools contained in this book, please visit www.thesagealliance.com/worksheets.

Articles

Sage Alliance offers a multitude of self-authored articles on leadership development and team optimization. Please visit http://thesagealliance.com/blog/ for a full list of offerings.

Please contact Shelley Hammell with Sage Alliance, Inc. at:

Email:
info@thesagealliance.com

LinkedIn:
https://www.linkedin.com/in/shelleyhammell

Facebook:
https://www.facebook.com/shelley.hammell

Twitter:
https://twitter.com/ShelleyHammell

You Tube:
https://www.youtube.com/channel/UCP_6z7NnInoof4WqyNkbqBg

Sign up for the Sage Alliance monthly newsletter at www.thesagealliance.com for up-to-date information, tips, and techniques for how you can optimize your leadership.

Who else in your company can benefit from the SAGE Coaching Approach to transform into a more effective leader coach?

To purchase multiple copies of this book for your leadership team, contact info@thesagealliance.com.

Additional Resources

There are several additional resources that will help you on your leadership journey.

Personality and Leadership Assessments

For more information on the assessments mentioned in this book, please refer to the links included in this section.

The Birkman Method:
https://birkman.com/

Everything DiSC Assessment:
https://www.wiley.com/

Herrmann Brain Dominance Instrument (HBDI):
https://www.herrmannsolutions.com/

Hogan Assessments:
https://www.hoganassessments.com/

Leadership Books

To continue developing as a leader coach, I have listed several leadership books I recommend reading.

Emotional Intelligence 2.0 by Travis Bradberry and Jean Greaves

StrengthsFinder 2.0 by Tom Rath

The Power of a Positive Team by Jon Gordon

Radical Candor by Kim Scott

The Four Obsessions of an Extraordinary Executive by Patrick Lencioni

The Five Temptations of a CEO by Patrick Lencioni

The Ideal Team Player by Patrick Lencioni

The 7 Habits of Highly Effective People by Stephen R. Covey

Fierce Conversations by Susan Scott

Crucial Conversations by Kerry Patterson, Joseph Grenny, Ron McMillan, Al Switzler

About the Author

Shelley Hammell is president and CEO of Sage Alliance, Inc., an Atlanta-based leadership-development company. Her real-world experience with executives, combined with her passion to help leaders gain greater self-awareness and zero in on what it takes to be more effective and build high-performing teams, was the impetus for starting her own company. She has coached and facilitated thousands of high-potential leaders worldwide to prepare them for their next role by assessing their impact and identifying the skills needed to operate at a more senior level and go from ordinary to extraordinary.

Previously as a vice president of global marketing, she hired, trained, and led international, cross-functional teams. She knows what it takes to grow top talent and deliver measurable results globally.

Shelley is a graduate of the Coaches Training Institute (CTI), the worldwide leader in coach training, and is certified in multiple assessment tools, including the Birkman, Herrmann Brain Dominance Instrument, Hogan Leadership Forecast Series, EQ Emotional Intelligence, and DiSC.

She has taught MBA students effective communication skills at the University of Georgia (UGA), has achieved the top 2 percent contributor for published articles on LinkedIn, and has been featured as on-air talent for Georgia Public Broadcasting (GPB-TV).

Her approach to coaching helps leaders inspire, empower, and advance their teams as they develop their own skills as effective leader coaches. Her expansive experience in coaching and leading workshops with Fortune 1000 clients enables her to understand the cultural nuances and leadership dimensions necessary to be successful in a global context.

Contact us with questions on how to implement a leader coaching approach in your organization, or to share your success stories: www.thesagealliance.com.